STREET NAMES OF MILTON KEYNES

STREET NAMES OF MILTON KEYNES
EAST

ANNE BAKER

Phillimore

2006

Published by
PHILLIMORE & CO. LTD
Shopwyke Manor Barn, Chichester, West Sussex, England
phillimore.co.uk

ISBN 1-86077-411-3
ISBN 13 978-1-86077-411-9

Printed and bound in Great Britain by
THE CROMWELL PRESS
Trowbridge, Wiltshire

CONTENTS

ACKNOWLEDGEMENTS

I would like to thank John Platt, former Secretary to the Board of Milton Keynes Development Corporation, for agreeing to write the Foreword to this book and, as the man originally charged with the task of naming the streets of the new city, making the project possible in the first place. Also, Liz Preston, Milton Keynes City Discovery Centre; Zena Flinn, the Living Archive, Wolverton and Ruth Meardon, the Local Studies Centre Milton Keynes Library. All those who provided photographs, including David Watts and staff of the Centre for Buckinghamshire Studies; Brett Thorn, Buckinghamshire Museum; Dankworth Management, Wavendon and Scott Grace. Geoffrey Dawes of Two Village Archive Trust for help with Milton Keynes village, Claire Grace and Ruth Cammies of the Open University Library and Archives and, last but not least, my husband John, who wrote the Introduction to this book and helped in so many ways before he died in November 2004.

Dedication

In memory of my husband
John Anthony Baker
1935-2004

FOREWORD

There is a wealth of history in the names in Milton Keynes. They act as a daily reminder of the people who lived in the area through the ages, their way of life, their use of the land and the skills and trades they practised. Sir Frank Markham, in his introduction to the first volume of his *History of Milton Keynes and District* (1973), hoped that the new generation in Milton Keynes might 'wish to know of its past, and to retain the best of it'. Sir Frank was a great believer in the continuity of communities and the value of roots. He had been an opponent of the proposal to build a new town in North Buckinghamshire, but, faced with the decision to go ahead, he and a number of other local people sought to engage with the planners in order to have new development complement the existing settlements. They were particularly anxious to see Stony Stratford and the villages incorporated into the new city in a form they would find acceptable and to make the new city something of which they, too, could be proud. Happily for all concerned, as Michael Reed, later one of the founding Directors of the City Discovery Centre, noted in *The Buckinghamshire Landscape* (1979), the Development Corporation took 'an enlightened attitude towards conservation'.

I remember back in 1973 Sir Frank and Lady Markham walking with Fred Roche, Stuart Mosscrop and Chris Woodward, round the area of the Secklow Mound and down the quiet green lane that ran from Bradwell Common to the Great Linford-Little Woolstone road. Sir Frank, who wanted to impress on the Corporation the long history of the area and the role of the Secklow Hundred as a 'centre of government', was greatly encouraged by the willingness of the designers to listen to his enthusiastic presentation of the past. One of those on this walk was a devotee of the theory of ley lines and would later propose the 'midsummer solstice' pattern of naming for the boulevards. Sir Frank wrote to me in October 1974, a year before he died, expressing the hope 'that my work may in some way help to produce a fine civic consciousness in the great new city'. He never saw the city centre, but I am sure he would have been delighted with the naming of the boulevards and with the incorporation of the Secklow Mound behind the Library.

The names found in Milton Keynes are by no means all from the growth of the new city. Areas like Bradwell, Fenny Stratford, Loughton and Stony Stratford, to name but a few, all contain road names from long before the designation of a new city. So, it was only sensible that, from the beginning, the Development Corporation should have taken naming seriously and welcomed, in 1968, an approach from Newport Pagnell RDC on the question of preserving the history of the area when identifying elements of the new city. Bob Dunbabin, the Clerk of Newport Pagnell RDC, and Ray Bellchambers, then a member of the RDC and a Corporation Board Member, were particularly keen to see the old merged into the new. The Corporation indicated its willingness to take the initiative on naming and I (with a more than passing interest in history) was deputed to do the work. The Local Authorities Joint Liaison Committee endorsed the proposal that the Corporation should take the lead and one of our first acts was to send Sue Godber to see Mr Shirley at Peartree Farm, Woughton-on-the-Green, to collect field names; Eaglestone was one of the fruits of this visit.

A small group of MKDC Board Members (Ray Bellchambers, Margaret Durbridge and Jim Cassidy), with a highways engineer (John Rowlands) and myself, devised and put forward the proposals for naming the city areas and the city's H and V roads, and the Board of the Development Corporation cleared the proposals before they were submitted to the local authorities, which had the legal responsibility for such matters. Nearly all the proposals made by the Corporation were accepted, although Wolverton UDC was not happy with the name Hodge Furze and requested a change to Hodge Lea. Those of us who liked the idea of naming the city centre Secklow were over-ruled before any proposals left the Corporation. The local authorities, particularly Newport Pagnell RDC and UDC and Wolverton UDC, played a very helpful part in the process, being keen to conserve all sensible links between the past and the new city's future. Bletchley UDC, which, in my view, was never very enthusiastic about the Development Corporation's role, was unwilling to see defined and named areas created within the UDC boundaries or to anticipate the naming and navigational needs of the wider city road system.

Naming the 'city roads' and CMK 'gates' was one opportunity to conserve long gone aspects of local history, such as Secklow (914), Snelshall Priory (12th century), the Portway (a 13th-century route to Newport), and Groveway (1781). I remember taking the name for Dansteed Way from Dansteed Furlong (Dunstead 1641), mentioned in the book *The Roman Roads of South-East England*. The archaeologists had not yet discovered an ancient settlement in the area – but there was indeed a 'place on the hill', as Dennis Mynard was later happy to tell me! If Dr Margaret Gelling had published her book *Place-Names in the Landscape* (1984) twenty years earlier, we would have been better equipped to spot more significant names from the past.

To 'name' an urban area the size of Milton Keynes was not an easy task. As the opening of new areas and the building of houses gathered pace, the co-operation of developers had to be sought. Some of them were wont to use unimaginative 'catalogue lists' of names for their schemes, which they repeated in towns all over the country. We were ably supported by the new Milton Keynes Borough Council in our efforts to broaden the developers' horizons, the Council sharing our desire to see varied and interesting names adopted. We sought to introduce 'different' themes, particularly in the early years. The Corporation broke new ground with the landscaping of Milton Keynes; we tried in our small way to bring some variety into the naming too.

Pleasing everybody is, of course, impossible, names being a matter of personal taste. It has to be borne in mind that even names low down in the order of things – such as a small residential close on the edge of Milton Keynes – have to be unique if confusion is to be avoided in postal and traffic terms. Producing around 2,000 of them between 1970 and 1992 was not easy; they all had to be cleared by the appropriate councillor as well as by the Council itself. Where did the new city's names come from? Well, many backgrounds, as Anne Baker has recorded so carefully. In the villages history was the usual basis and the Heritage Map (1983), compiled by Bob Croft and Brian Giggins, shows the background to some of the historical names used in the city. Elsewhere themes were selected from which suitable names could emerge, as at Heelands where it was decided to use names from the North-West Yorkshire Highlands, an area with which one of those responsible had a personal family link. Myrtle Bank (Stacey Bushes) reminded me of a hotel in Kingston, Jamaica. Other names were reminiscent of far-flung places known to those involved (in one case a distant holiday home). The 'rock stars' theme at Crownhill was suggested by a local resident who was a member of the Elvis Presley Fan Club, Elvis being 'the King'. Ray Bellchambers made a number of suggestions for names in the Stantonbury and Bradwell areas. The names in Campbell Park were selected in appreciation of the role of Lord Campbell of Eskan in the development of Milton Keynes. Many people made contributions to the bank of names.

Sometimes there were objections. One university-educated resident complained to Wolverton UDC that the name 'Blackdown' at Fullers Slade had unfortunate racial connotations and was unacceptable; he was apparently unaware that the theme was hills and that the Blackdown Hills are in Devon. On another occasion I was asked why such a boringly ordinary name as 'William Smith Close' was used at Woolstone; explanation of the importance of William Smith and his steam plough put that right. Milton Keynes Parish Council invited me to a meeting to explain why such unknown and irrelevant names had been put forward for their village; again, explanation of the historical context of the names was accepted by the villagers. A sign of the times was a reluctance in the early 1970s to see one name attached to a road with both rental and sale housing schemes on it – or even to see the schemes sharing the same access road! By the 1980s such views had disappeared. At Kiln Farm, where the names were in place before many occupants arrived, I received a strong reaction to the spine road being called 'Pitfield'; in this case, the names had been officially approved, but I was told in very straight terms how detrimental to marketing a name like 'Pitfield' would be. I still cannot see the problem (it was after all an old brickmaking area, hence Brickkiln Farm). No London banks seemed to find an address in 'Cheapside' a disadvantage.

One of the last naming tasks I undertook personally, together with highways engineer John Wardley, was the naming of the city road roundabouts. If anyone I meet – in places far from Milton Keynes – has been to the new city, it is the roundabouts they talk about. Despite the Corporation's Information Unit producing city road maps from 1975 and placing Information Boards (incorporating maps) in lay-bys at the entrances to the Designated Area from 1976, the H and V roads and the roundabouts have always defeated some sections of society. We discovered early in the development that lorry drivers mastered map-reading and the navigation system fairly quickly, but those with high-powered cars or higher education found them difficult!

It is hard to believe that it is nearly forty years since the new city project began and it is heartening to see a book incorporating the results of what was essentially a 'backroom' task among the complex and highly technical responsibilities of the Development Corporation. It would be remiss of me not to take the opportunity to acknowledge the contributions made by Ralph Bailey (BMK) and Teresa Jenkins and Val Sharpe (MKDC) over a long period. In addition to their real jobs, they coped with the naming of roads in a multitude of housing developments throughout the new city – a sometimes thankless task, although fascinating to look back on. I also remember well the kindness and support received in the early days from the late Colin Rees, when he was Wolverton UDC's Chief Engineer, and the co-operation received over many years from Dennis Mynard and the staff of the Archaeology Unit.

JOHN PLATT
Secretary to the Board of the
Milton Keynes Development Corporation 1983-92

INTRODUCTION
by John Baker

When in 1967 nearly forty square miles of North Buckinghamshire countryside was designated for the building of Britain's biggest New Town, it was a decision which stirred the emotions of people then living in the three towns and 13 villages in the area.

Many people, particularly those in the northern towns of Wolverton and Stony Stratford, were totally opposed to the concept. Ten miles south, however, the majority of Bletchley residents were far more welcoming, living as they did under an urban authority which had been involved in building 'overspill' accommodation, mainly for Londoners, since shortly after the end of the Second World War.

In 1962, Buckinghamshire's chief architect and planning officer, Fred Pooley, had produced proposals for a city in which the transport system would be based on a monorail with townships of up to 7,000 people built along the route and with no homes more than seven minutes' walk from a station. The object of Pooley's vision was instantly tagged 'Pooleyville' by the local press.

It has been said that Pooley's vision 'laid the foundations' for a future city, although initially it produced considerable squabbling among national, county and local politicians during the early years of the 1960s. This makes it all the more surprising to recall that, by early 1966, the concept finally came into focus in the shape of a map produced by Richard Crossman, Labour's Minister of Housing and Local Government at that time. It revealed an area (later reduced after a public inquiry to 21,900 acres, roughly 34 square miles) on which it was planned to build the biggest New Town of them all, with a population of a quarter of a million people.

Suddenly, speed was of the essence.

Within a matter of months, the Draft North Buckinghamshire New Town (Designation Order) was made and announced by Anthony Greenwood, who had succeeded Crossman. The name Milton Keynes was chosen from one of the villages in the area – a choice strongly supported by Lord Campbell of Eskan, the first appointed Chairman of Milton Keynes Development Corporation, as acknowledging the hybrid of the poet Milton and the internationally acclaimed economist, John Maynard Keynes.

With the appointment of the Main Consultants, Llewelyn-Davies Weeks Forestier-Walker and Bor, and members of the Board of the Corporation, concentration was focused on establishing the key issues affecting the widest range of planning and social objectives, the goals of architects and engineers, the search for vital decisions over the vexed question of the city's transport system, projected housing densities and the siting and size of the new main shopping centre.

Problems on a scale never before encountered were overcome, one by one, as a direct result of the involvement of many of the country's finest planners, architects and engineers gathered together by a Corporation determined to meet the challenges and opportunities presented to make the venture the success it has undoubtedly become.

The Plan for Milton Keynes, which followed an Interim Report a year earlier, was produced for limited distribution among Board members and senior officers late in 1969. Its two volumes were formally launched at a press conference the following March and a Public Inquiry, lasting ten days, took place towards the end of June.

Opposition to the Plan had by now largely dissipated as work began on putting in the first phases of the city's infrastructure. The grid road system as we know it today, started with a section of the H2 (Millers Way) east of the V7 (Saxon Street), there were presentations of plans for specific areas, the first MKDC housing schemes got underway at Simpson and in Stony Stratford, the Open University arrived at Walton Hall, and proposals for the central area of Bletchley and for the two northern towns were presented.

It was all systems go. Then came the shock announcement that the little village of Cublington, near Wing, had been listed among the possible sites for the third London airport. The impact of this news sent shockwaves through most people living in North Buckinghamshire. A poll conducted by the *Milton Keynes Gazette* revealed that more than 90 per cent opposed the plan, which would also have the effect of turning Milton Keynes into an airport city.

The Hon. Mr Justice Roskill, chairing the Commission of Inquiry into the siting of the airport, published plans which would lead to the expansion of Milton Keynes westwards from Bletchley, through Winslow, to provide for a population of more than 400,000 people.

Lord Campbell, who was to earn the soubriquet of 'the father of Milton Keynes', led the fight, strongly supported by press and public, against the proposal which became, for him, a resignation issue. In evidence to the Commission, he went as far as to suggest that grafting an airport onto that part of Milton Keynes which would have been developed by 1987, 'could only produce a mongrel city'. He was subsequently joined in opposition by Professor Colin Buchanan, an architect and town planner who was also a Commission member. His dissenting report ultimately saved the city as we know it today.

Cublington was dropped by the government from the list of possible sites in April 1971 and over the past two decades the plan has become reality.

Development on this scale could only have come about as a result of the participants' belief in the Plan and their collective and individual belief in their abilities, led by a man who was a passionate believer in Milton Keynes.

THE GRID ROADS

The main thoroughfares through Milton Keynes are designed in the pattern of a grid, each square enclosing an estate. The grid roads are numbered vertically – V 1-11 called Streets, and horizontally – H 1-10 called Ways. Even before Roman times, there were several ancient trackways crossing the area which is now Milton Keynes, particularly from west to east, and most of the H Ways have taken their names.

Snelshall Street (V 1)   Refers to Snelshall Priory which stood about a mile and a half to the south-west of nearby Whaddon church. The priory was founded in about 1219 and stood in 11 acres of surrounding countryside.

Tattenhoe Street (V 2)   Named after the tiny village of Tattenhoe, now incorporated in the Tattenhoe area of Milton Keynes. The site of the Norman homestead of Tattenhoe has been preserved.

Fulmer Street (V 3)   Meaning 'the foul mere', Fulmer takes its name from an ancient pond at Shenley Brook End. Also, Fulmoor Close is marked on a 1771 Plan and Survey of Shenley as a field owned by William Brice.

Watling Street (V 4)   This is the section of the old Roman road between Fenny Stratford and Stony Stratford. Until the arrival of Milton Keynes, it was a stretch of the A5 until a new section of the A5 was constructed in the 1970s so that through traffic could have an uninterrupted passage through the new city. The name Watling Street derives from the ninth-century *Waeclinga straet,* meaning 'a Roman road identified with the followers of a man called Wacol', believed to have been centred around St Albans, an early name for which was *Waeclingaceaster.*

Great Monks Street (V 5)   Passes by Bradwell Abbey following the route of an old track along which the monks once traversed.

Grafton Street (V 6)   In the 18th century the Dukes of Grafton (family name Fitzroy) held substantial lands and property in south Northamptonshire, owning several local villages including Deanshanger and Paulerspury. They had a great mansion, Wakefield Lodge, near Potterspury, about a mile from Stony Stratford, where, according to Frank Markham in his *History of Milton Keynes and District*, the Graftons did most of their shopping and tipped the tradesmen with braces of pheasant or partridge. Descended from Charles II, the 3rd Duke was Prime Minister 1768-9 and the 4th Duke (1821-1918) was a well-known local figure.

Saxon Street (V 7)   This street leads to and passes through the centre of Milton Keynes, which is built at the highest point in the area and on the site of Secklow Corner, the ancient Saxon meeting place of the Secklow Hundred.

Marlborough Street (V 8)   The Dukes of Marlborough were associated with the Milton Keynes area after Sarah, Duchess of Marlborough purchased the Stantonbury estates in 1727. She gave it to her grandson, John Spencer, and the lands remained in the ownership of the Earls Spencer of Althorp, Northamptonshire until well into the 19th century. Marlborough Street begins at Stantonbury and skirts the east side of the modern estate.

Overstreet (V 9)   Following the line of a 17th-century track near Downs Barn, this is a short stretch of carriageway connecting Campbell Park with Great Linford. The affix *Over* usually indicates a place 'at the ridge or slope'.

Brickhill Street (V 10)   Named after the villages of Little, Great and Bow Brickhill from where this street begins on its journey northwards to meet the Wolverton road at Great Linford. It replaces an ancient road which ran beside the river Ouzel to Danesborough, an historic hill fort in the woods above Bow Brickhill. According to the *Oxford Dictionary of English Place Names,* Brickhill has nothing to do with bricks, but derives from the Celtic *brig* meaning 'hill top' and the Old English *hyll.*

Tongwell Street (V 11)   Named after the field on which stood Tongwell Farm, shown on an 1806 map of Newport Pagnell. Tongwell Street runs from Old Farm Park to the outskirts of Newport Pagnell.

Ridgeway (H 1)   This is a short section of the prehistoric Ridgeway track which ran from Avebury on Salisbury Plain to the east coast at the Wash.

Millers Way (H 2)   This was the first of the new city roads to be built. It follows the line of an old track which ran between Bradwell windmill and Stony Stratford, hence the name Millers Way.

Monks Way (H 3)   Skirting the site of Bradwell Abbey, this name refers to the monks which once inhabited the abbey and traversed the tracks and pathways in the area.

Dansteed Way (H 4)   Danstead was an ancient site and field name, 'Long Danstead and Short Danstead', shown on a 1678 plan of the area. It is tempting to suggest that the site may have been a homestead occupied by the Danes, but excavations carried out in 1979-81 revealed it to be the site of an Iron-Age/Saxon village. There were, however, many savage raids by the Danes in the early 1000s AD, including an invasion of Newport Pagnell, and several Danish settlements in the area now covered by Milton Keynes. The road runs from Grange Farm in the west to Newport Pagnell.

Portway (H 5)   A Roman route running from Whaddon, through Shenley and Seckloe, to Willen was known by AD 1250 as 'Rector's Portway', and 'Dichefurlong by Portwei'. The new thoroughfare which has taken its name follows close to the old track. Port, meaning a town, or market town, identifies this as 'the way to town' i.e. Newport Pagnell.

Childs Way (H 6)   This takes its name from an 18th-century track and field name in east Loughton, by which the road passes on its way from Shenley Common Farm in the east to the M1 at junction 14. An archaic meaning of child (or childe) was a young nobleman. Alternatively, someone named Child(s) may have owned or farmed land in Loughton.

Chaffron Way (H 7)   This was the name of an 18th-century track through Woughton, by which the modern Chaffron Way passes. A chaffron, or chamfron, is a piece of leather or plate of steel worn by a horse to protect its face in battle. The reason for its use here is obscure.

Standing Way (H 8)   This follows the route of an ancient track which, it is believed, linked Buckingham, via Thornborough, to Watling Street and the Roman station of Magiovinium near Fenny Stratford. Today it is the A421, which runs from Buckingham to the A1, east of Bedford. The name Standing may be a derivation of the Old English word *staning* meaning 'stony places'.

Groveway (H 9)   Groveway has been in existence and called by this name since at least the 18th century. It travels from Watling Street at Bletchley to the north side of Wavendon, where it gives way to the ancient London road, coming in from Hockliffe, through Woburn and on to Newport Pagnell. Presumably it once passed through the groves of walnut and other trees which grew in this area.

Bletcham Way (H 10)   This was the name of another 18th-century track which passed through Woughton. The name derives from *Blecca's-ham*, the Old English meaning 'homestead of a man called Blecca'. The present road runs from Bletchley to Wavendon Gate.

A Note on OS Map References

The Ordnance Survey (OS) numbers referred to are taken from the Milton Keynes Development Corporation's paper *Names in Milton Keynes* (1992) and are from a 1:2500 scale edition updated in 1965. A collection of old maps may be seen, by appointment, at Milton Keynes City Discovery Centre, Bradwell Abbey, or at the Local Studies Centre, Central Milton Keynes Library.

ATTERBURY

In 1656, Oliver Cromwell presented the Reverend Lewis Atterbury to the rectorate of the church of All Saints, Milton Keynes. Anxious for his position after the Restoration in 1660, he went to plead his case at the Royal Court in London. His fears proved unfounded for not only was

The Rev. Lewis Atterbury, rector of All Saints' church, 1657-c.1692.

his Milton Keynes title sanctioned but he was also made chaplain to Charles II's son, the Duke of Gloucester. However, he spent years fighting a legal battle to recover the Milton Keynes glebe lands which had been sequestered during the Civil War. He was drowned in 1691 while trying to cross a bridge during a flood in Newport Pagnell. His son, Francis Atterbury, born at Milton Keynes in 1663, was also a prelate who was ordained in 1687 and whose preachings were so highly regarded that he was appointed lecturer of St Bride's, a royal chaplain and minister to Bridewell Hospital. By 1713, he was Bishop of Rochester and Dean of Westminster but, because of his Jacobite leanings, fell out of favour with George I and was committed to the Tower for complying with an attempt to restore the Stuart monarchy. He was stripped of all his offices and banished from the country. He died in Paris in 1732 and is buried in an unnamed grave in Westminster Abbey. This estate is still under construction.

THEME **Steam Railways**

Bressingham Gate   Bressingham Steam Museum and Gardens near Diss in Norfolk has a collection of standard gauge locomotives which includes the famous LMS *Royal Scot*, which is under restoration, and a collection of narrow gauge engines which includes an exact replica of the *Flying Scotsman*.

Fairbourne Drive   The Fairbourne & Barmouth Narrow Gauge Steam Railway is near Dolgellau in Wales. The trains run round the bay from Fairbourne station to Penrhyn Point and on the way pass through the station with the longest name in the world, which is Gorsafawddachairdraigodanheddogleddollonpenrhynareurdraethceredigion. It means 'The Mawddach station with its dragon's teeth on the northerly Penrhyn drive on the golden beach of Cardigan Bay'. The railway was first laid in 1895 by Arthur McDougall, the flour manufacturer, and was used to carry construction materials for the building of Fairbourne village. The original 15-inch gauge was changed to 12¼ inches in 1985.

Wansford Avenue Wansford station near Peterborough is the headquarters of the Nene Valley Railway. It is a picturesque village by the river with 18th-century granaries which have been converted into cottages and the remains of a paper mill which closed in 1855. The standard gauge railway line runs seven-and-a-half miles along the Nene Valley between Yarwell Junction and Peterborough, passing through Wansford station, where there is a collection of steam locomotives and coaches from all over Europe and Britain.

BLAKELANDS

The name Blakelands is possibly from the Anglo-Saxon 'bleak' or 'desolate' lands. It was an existing name of a field shown west of the M1 on Ordnance Survey map 14 and map of Newport Pagnell dated 1806.

THEME **The Industrial Revolution**

Bessemer Court Thanks to Sir Henry Bessemer (1813-98), Britain became the world's leading steel producer. An engineer born in Hertfordshire, he discovered that steel could be made faster and more cheaply by pumping a blast of air into pig iron. His name was given to the Bessemer Converter in which the process was carried out, which was used by the British Steel Corporation until 1977.

Hargreaves Nook James Hargreaves (1720-78) of Blackburn, Lancashire was an illiterate weaver and carpenter who invented the 'Spinning Jenny'. This was a spinning machine which enabled one man to operate several spinning wheels at once. From 1764, the Jenny revolutionised cloth weaving in England, but as it could do the work of 30 men it greatly upset the workers. Some of the spinners smashed up his frame and his home and drove him out of Lancashire. He set up a small mill in Nottinghamshire manufacturing yarn, but died an unsung hero and a poor man.

Huntsman Grove Benjamin Huntsman (1705-76) was a Quaker and clockmaker from Sheffield. He carried out experiments to find a better material for the springs of clocks and pendulums and found a method for producing cast steel in small clay crucibles, which became known as Huntsman crucible steel. It was used in the cutlery making industry, both in Sheffield and abroad.

Metcalfe Grove   From 1765, John Metcalf (1717-1810) built 185 miles of road and hundreds of bridges in Yorkshire and Lancashire. He was blind from the age of six and became known as 'Blind Jack of Knaresborough'. Nevertheless, he grew into a tall, energetic man, managed to drive a stagecoach, was involved in smuggling and, apparently, fought at Culloden and Falkirk.

Minton Close   Thomas Minton (1765-1836) founded his porcelain factory in 1796 at Stoke-on-Trent. His Minton ware is valued for its artistic elegance. Born in Shrewsbury, Thomas first worked as a transfer-print engraver and was employed by the Spode factory before setting up his own works. Here he produced copper plates for transfer-printing in blue underglaze. He is credited with having invented the willow pattern. In 1793 he built a pottery at Stoke and turned to making fine bone china, mostly table ware decorated with painted flowers and fruit.

Smeaton Close   John Smeaton (1724-94) is considered to be the first fully professional civil engineer. He was the first to realise the combined efficiency of wind, water and steam as sources of energy, which he demonstrated through his precise experiments. As a boy he made his own tools and built model machines. His interest in scientific instruments led him to set up his own business, inventing navigational instruments which he submitted to the Royal Society. Aged only 29, in 1753 he was elected a Fellow of the Society. Through his engineering skills, he won the contract to build a new Eddystone lighthouse. Completed in 1759, it is the masterpiece for which he is best known.

Tanners Drive   Leading to the large industrial area of Blakelands, this road takes the old name of a field which may have had some connection with the tanning industry.

Telford Way   Thomas Telford (1757-1834) was the son of a Scottish shepherd. Aged 13 he was apprenticed to a stone mason. Later he moved to London where he worked on the building of Somerset House while studying civil engineering and architecture. Returning to Scotland, he engineered a completely new road network for the country. He also designed and built hundreds of bridges, improved harbours and docks and built the Caledonian Canal. The Menai Suspension Bridge, connecting the North Wales mainland to Anglesey, is his greatest achievement.

Wedgwood Avenue   Josiah Wedgwood, the English potter, was born at Burslem in 1730. His cream-coloured Queen's ware was first patented in 1763. The unglazed blue Jasper ware and black basalt ware followed and by 1769 he had established a new pottery at Hanley which he named 'Etruria' after an ancient Italian state. Here he made pots, jugs and vases in ancient classical styles and built a complete village for his workmen. More than a potter, Josiah Wedgwood was a leading figure among the 18th-century industrialists who contributed capital and encouraged the technological innovation which turned the wheels of the Industrial Revolution. He was involved in the development of new turnpike roads and was a key figure in the formation of the Grand Junction Canal Company and in the canal's construction, which was beneficial to the smooth transportation of his china ware. He died in 1795.

Yeomans Drive   This is also named after a field, which possibly belonged to the yeoman, a member of a class of small freeholders who cultivated their own land.

BOLBECK PARK

Bolbeck Park, in the old parish of Great Linford, is named after Hugh de Bolebec who held the manor of Linford in 1066. He was a relative of Walter Giffard, and came to England at the time of the Norman Conquest from Bolbec, near Le Havre in Normandy.

THEME **The Norman Conquest**

Bec Lane   Bec was a monastery built by Lanfranc. It was one of many monasteries which sprang up as centres of religion and learning in the early 11th century as part of a strong movement of reform in northern Europe.

Bernay Gardens   Bernay, south-west of Rouen in Normandy, is the site of a major 11th-century abbey founded by an Italian, William of Volpiano. The Benedictine Abbey Church of Notre Dame, built 1050-60, still stands and the town has many quaint old houses.

Falaise Nook   Falaise in Normandy was the birthplace of William I (the Conqueror) and site of the castles of the dukes of Normandy. The town was destroyed during the Normandy campaign of the Second World War when, on 7 July 1944, the RAF dropped 2,500 tons of bombs. In the summer of that year, the battle of the Falaise Gap was fought over 800 miles of countryside and lasted for two weeks.

Flambard Close   Ralph Flambard succeeded Lanfranc as chief adviser to William I after Lanfranc was appointed Archbishop of Canterbury.

Lacy Drive   Walter de Lacy, from Lassy in Calvados, came to England with William I's conquering army in 1066. He was given lands and an earldom in Herefordshire and was an important defender against the Welsh. He helped to crush a rebellion by Earl William FitzOsburn's son, Roger. He died in 1085 and was succeeded by his son Roger.

Lanfranc Gardens   Lanfranc (*c.*1005-89) was an Italian churchman and theologian who, in 1043, founded and became prior of the Benedictine

Abbey at Bec in Normandy. In 1062 he became Prior of St Stephen's Abbey at Caen. He came to England with William the Conqueror, who appointed him Archbishop of Canterbury in 1070. He also acted as one of William's political advisers.

Lascelles Close   The Lascelles family came to Britain from Normandy at the time of the Conquest. The name derives from their place of origin, the town of Lacelle, near Alençon in the Orne district of Normandy.

Montgomery Crescent   Roger de Montgomery was a powerful and wealthy Norman who contributed 60 ships to William the Conqueror's invasion fleet. He was appointed by William to take care of Normandy during his absence on the invasion of England. Montgomery came to Britain in 1067 and was given the earldoms of Shrewsbury and Arundel, which included the lordships of 84 manors. He founded the first castle at Arundel on Christmas Day 1067, the same day that William was crowned king. His ghost is said to haunt the keep of the castle. It is a coincidence that the Commander-in-Chief of the British and Allied Armies during the 1944 invasion of Normandy was Viscount Montgomery of Alamein (Bernard Law Montgomery, 1887-1976).

Orne Gardens   The river Orne flows through the city of Caen in Normandy and reaches the English Channel at what, on 6 June 1944, formed part of the Sword Beach landing area during the Normandy invasion by British and Canadian troops.

Redvers Gate   The Redvers family came to Britain from Normandy at the time of the Conquest. Richard de Redvers, son of Baldwin de Brioncis, was a baron in the court of William I and was created Earl of Devon by Henry I.

St Stephen's Drive   Named after St Stephen's monastery at Caen in Normandy. Lanfranc was prior there before coming to England with William I. A new abbey church was built in about 1050-70.

Venables Lane   Gilbert de Venables came from Venables, near Evreux in Normandy. He is believed to have fought at the Battle of Hastings and was rewarded with the barony of Kinderton in Cheshire and the lands which went with it.

Wavell Court   The Wavell family came to England from Normandy at the time of the Conquest. The name derives from their place of origin, Vauville in Manche, Normandy.

BRINKLOW

Brinklow Hills was the name of a field in this south-east corner of Milton Keynes, shown on a 1685 Milton Keynes map, Ordnance Survey 10. On a map of Simpson in 1781, showing the estate of Sir Walden Hanmer, Joseph Brinklow is identified as a farmer with land there. No doubt a descendant of the same family, A.C. Brinklow had a newsagent's shop in Fenny Stratford until the 1960s. Little more than a mile from junctions 13 and 14 of the M1, modern Brinklow is mainly used for warehousing. The four roads here are named after trustees of the Stony Stratford to Hockliffe Turnpike, about whom nothing is known except that they would have been reputable local citizens appointed as commissioners responsible for the upkeep of this particular turnpike road.

Bransworth Avenue   Mr Nehemiah Bransworth was a trustee in 1706.

Brudenell Drive   Mr Thomas Brudenell was a 1739 trustee.

Etheridge Avenue   William Etheridge was a trustee in 1739.

Harding Road   The Rev. Harding was clerk of the Turnpike Trust in 1706 and 1739.

BROUGHTON

One of the 13 original villages and one of the last to be swallowed whole by the development of Milton Keynes, Broughton nevertheless manages to retain much of its ancient dignity by virtue of its peripheral position.

THEME **Local History and Steam Railways**

Ambergate   In the Amber Valley, Derbyshire, the main Midland Railway line once ran between Pye Bridge and Ambergate. The preservation of the last section of the line was prevented by the construction of the A38.

Ardley Mews   The village of Ardley lies just off junction 10 of the M40, between Banbury and Bicester and close to the railway line. It appears to have no special connection with steam railways, and its main claim to fame is the numerous dinosaur footprints recently found covering the floor of Ardley limestone quarries, including that of Megalosaurus of the Jurassic period.

Bewdley Grove   Bewdley is a main station on the Severn Valley Railway, which runs for 16 miles from Kidderminster in Worcestershire to

Bridgnorth, Shropshire. Saved from obscurity by a group of enthusiasts, it is a full-size, standard gauge line with restored passenger trains hauled by steam locomotives. At Bewdley there is a large collection of working steam engines and coaches, some of which are more than 80 years old.

Early 14th-century St Lawrence's church, Broughton, which has some preserved wall paintings.

Bulmer Close Bulmer Railway Centre at Hereford houses a collection of steam locomotives and rolling stock.

Cadeby Court Cadeby Light Railway and Brass Rubbings Centre is at Market Bosworth, Leicestershire. Its narrow gauge steam railway, miniature and model railways and related attractions won the 1990 Country Heritage award.

Eskdale Way In Cumbria, the Ravenglass to Eskdale Steam Railway was opened in 1875 to carry iron ore, granite and copper from the mines and quarries near Boot in Eskdale to the estuary at Ravenglass. A year later it also carried passengers. In 1913 the 3ft-gauge track was closed but an enthusiastic model-maker, Mr Bassett-Lowke, took it over and reopened it in 1914 with a 15-inch gauge. The miniature railway carried goods and passengers up until it closed again in 1953. It was then bought by enthusiasts at an auction sale in 1960 and is now a major tourist attraction in the region.

Highley Grove Highley in Shropshire is a small town with a station on the Severn Valley Railway line, midway between Kidderminster and Bridgnorth. Between 1874, when Highley Mining Company opened a colliery there, and 1969, when it closed, Highley was a thriving mining community and the long streets of miners cottages still survive. The station was opened in 1862 and Severn Valley Country Park spreads over the site of the old colliery.

Hunsbury Chase The Northamptonshire Ironstone Railway Trust and Industrial Museum at Hunsbury Hill Country Park was established in 1974 on the site of former ironstone workings. Among its collection of steam and diesel engines and rolling stock under restoration is Britain's only double-decker train. A demonstration standard gauge railway line runs for about a mile and a half round the park and there are passenger rides on Sundays and bank holidays.

Kidderminster Walk In Worcestershire, Kidderminster station is the starting point of the Severn Valley Railway's 16-mile journey to Bridgnorth

Cottages beside the old London Road through Broughton.

in Shropshire. As well as the collection of historic locomotives, the main stations on the line, such as Kidderminster, are proud of their catering facilities and Sunday luncheon trains run on most Sundays throughout the year.

London Road   Described in 1948 as a 'very main-road ridden brick village' (*Murray's Buckinghamshire Architectural Guide*), Broughton then stood on what was historically known as 'the Great Road to London'. It ran, as it still does for the most part, from the Watling Street at Hockliffe to Northampton, passing through Woburn, Wavendon, Broughton and Newport Pagnell. Realignment of this section of the road in the 1970s left Broughton cosily enclosed behind a screen of tall trees and the old London Road running into a cul-de-sac.

Milton Road   This is part of the old lane which ran from Broughton to the village of Milton Keynes.

Oakworth Avenue   Oakworth station, on the Keighley and Worth Valley Railway, West Yorkshire, was featured in the 1970 film production of *The Railway Children*. The station's stardom greatly improved the line's popularity, attracting a huge increase in passengers. The working line closed in 1962 and was acquired in 1965 by the Keighley and Worth Valley. It has won the Best Restored Station competition several times.

Ravenglass Croft   Ravenglass, on the estuary of the Esk, Mite and Irt rivers, is the only coastal town in the Lake District and was a Roman naval base in the second century. From here the narrow gauge steam trains of the Ravenglass to Eskdale Steam Railway carry passengers through two beautiful valleys to the foot of the highest hills in England.

Swanwick Lane   The Midland Railway Centre and Museum at Swanwick in Derbyshire is about a mile from junction 28 off the M1. It was set up in the

1970s as an industrial memorial to the Midland Railway's locomotive and coach works, which were built at Derby in the 1840s. Swanwick Junction station is undergoing restoration and the old Swanwick Colliery branch line is being adapted for passenger trains. There is also a Swanwick Junction model railway.

Tanfield Lane   The original Tanfield Railway line was built as early as 1647 as a means of carrying coal from the Durham mines to ships on the river Tyne. It was a huge engineering feat for its day, involving the building of several bridges, of which the Causey Arch across the Causey Burn survives. The track was made of wood and the wagons were pulled by horses until 1725 when iron and locomotives modernised the line. Never a passenger line, it carried coal until 1964. Preserved and restored by enthusiasts in the 1970s, a three-mile section still runs from Sunniside to East Tanfield, via Marley Hill and Causey Arch. About 40 rescued locomotives can be seen in various states of working order.

The Circus   A circus is an open space where several streets converge.

BROWNS WOOD

Browns Wood is named after the wood at Bow Brickhill and the wood was probably named after Sir Francis Brown, who was lord of the manor of Bow Brickhill from 1626 to about 1690.

THEME Composers of Classical Music

Bantock Close   Sir Granville Bantock (1868-1946) was an English composer born in London. He was Professor of Music at Birmingham University between 1908 and 1934 and was knighted in 1930. His musical inspiration was drawn from Oriental life, as shown in his *Omar Khayyam*. He also wrote choral works which include *Atlanta in Calydon* and *Hebridean Symphony*.

Bernstein Close   Leonard Bernstein (1918-90) was an American composer, conductor and pianist. He came to fame suddenly in 1943 when he was asked at very short notice to conduct the New York Philharmonic as a substitute for Bruno Walter, who had been taken ill. In 1958 he was appointed musical director of that orchestra. He is known as a composer who bridged the gap between serious and light music, having written two symphonies, ballet, film scores and musicals such as *West Side Story*.

Berwald Close   Franz Adolf Berwald (1796-1868) was a Swedish composer who played the violin and viola in the Swedish Court Orchestra. He composed four symphonies during the 1840s. He found the Swedish musical establishment too constricting so went abroad. When he returned to Sweden in 1849, he was passed over for two prestigious conductorships and worked instead as manager of a glass factory. A year before his death he was made Professor of Composition at the Swedish Royal Academy. Berwald composed operas, operettas and chamber music, but his work was not fully appreciated until it was rediscovered in the 20th century.

Bliss Court   Sir Arthur Bliss was born in London in 1891 of American parents and lived much of his life in the USA. He was educated at Rugby and Cambridge and the Royal College of Music. During the Second World War he was an administrator at the BBC and became Director of Music. He was appointed Master of the Queen's Musick in 1953. Some of Bliss's early works were unconventional, but later he became more traditionally English. In the latter part of his life he wrote illustrative music and three ballets: *Checkmate, Miracle in the Gorbals* and *Adam Zero*. His film scores included *Things to Come* and *Men of Two Worlds*. He also wrote choral and orchestral works. Bliss died in London in 1975.

Bowen Close   York Bowen was an English composer of piano music and a virtuoso pianist. He wrote a huge number of preludes, ballads and sonatas, composing the music he loved regardless of the requirements of musical fashion. He also played the viola and wrote *Fantasies for Four Violas* in 1907. Although he was one of England's greatest pianists, York Bowen has largely been forgotten.

Copeland Close   Aaron Copland (1900-90) was an American composer, born in Brooklyn, New York. His best-known music is based on American tradition and folk music. He wrote the ballets *Billy the Kid* and *Appalachian Spring,* which won the Pulitzer Prize in 1945, and composed impressive film scores. His other works include two operas, three symphonies, the ballet score for *Rodeo* and *Fanfare for the Common Man.* Copland was also a pianist and conductor. He stopped composing in 1970, but continued to lecture and conduct into the mid-1980s.

Delius Close   Frederick Delius, born in Bradford in 1862, was the son of a wealthy Prussian industrialist who had settled there. In 1882, Frederick rebelled against his father and left home to run an orange plantation in Florida. There, negro spirituals awakened his musical calling. He trained in Leipzig, where he met Grieg, and began composing. He moved to Paris and travelled widely across Europe and Scandinavia, and much of his music is evocative of the places he visited, for example *Paris, the Song of a Great City*. He spent the Second World War in England and wrote *A Song of the High Hills*. Delius died of syphilis in France in 1934, but his remains were later reburied in a south of England churchyard. He is known as a 'poet of nature', an impressionist who wrote tone poems such as *On Hearing the First Cuckoo in Spring* and *In a Summer Garden.*

Duparc Close   Henri Duparc (1848-1933) was a French composer, remembered for the songs written over the last 15 years of his life. There were only 17 of them, but they rank among the world's greatest. He studied under Cesar Franck and in his earlier years composed a violoncello sonata and other instrumental works which he later destroyed. An extremely emotional and self-critical man, he gave up composing at the age of 37.

Elgar Grove   Edward Elgar (1857-1934) was an English composer, organist and violinist from Worcestershire. He was the son of a musical father and wrote choral music such as *The Dream of Gerontius*, overtures, including *Cockaigne*, and is best known for his *Pomp and Circumstance March*, played every year at the 'Proms', *Enigma Variations* and his *'Cello Concerto*, so memorably played by the late Jacqueline du Pré.

Gabriel Close   Felix Godin Gabriel was a 16th-century composer whose works can now only be found as part of multi-composer collections. These include *In a Spanish Palace Songbook* and *The Voices in the Garden*, a collection of Spanish songs and motets 1480-1550. Both are recorded by Hyperion; the original *Spanish Palace* has been preserved for 500 years in the Royal Palace in Madrid.

Gershwin Court   George Gershwin was born in New York in 1898 and died in Hollywood in 1937. His father was a Russian Jew. He studied to become a concert pianist but his real interest lay in jazz and popular music. Leaving school at 15, he became a staff pianist with the Tin Pan Alley firm of Jerome H. Rimick & Co. and started song writing. Gershwin built himself a reputation as a composer for the theatre and established his name with songs like *Swanee*, sung by Al Jolson, and *I'll Build a Stairway to Paradise*. His jazz concerto *Rhapsody in Blue* and shows such as *Porgy and Bess* and *Lady Be Good*, starring Fred Astaire, are well known.

Holst Crescent   Gustav Holst (1874-1934) was an English composer of Swedish origin, born in Cheltenham. He suffered neuritis in his hand, which prevented him becoming a concert pianist, and instead played the trombone and joined the Scottish Orchestra. In 1905 he became music master at St Paul's Girls School in London, moving in 1907 to Morley College, where he was Director of Music, and again in 1911 to Reading College. It took Holst some time to find his own composing style. He is best known for his seven-movement suite *The Planets*, which confirmed him as a major composer. Other works include *The Hymn of Jesus, Ode to Death,* two comic operas and much more. He suffered from poor health and depression in later life.

Ireland Close   John Ireland (1879-1962) was an English composer, son of a Manchester bookseller, whose music was of a poetic nature, inspired by ancient traditions and places. He wrote an orchestral prelude, *The Forgotten Rite*, which was inspired by the Channel Islands, and a rhapsody of the Wessex countryside, *Mai-Dun*. His later works include song settings of poems by Thomas Hardy, Masefield, Housman and others. *These Things*

Shall Be was composed in honour of the Coronation of George VI. Ireland's last days were spent in a Sussex windmill, where he died aged 81.

Mahler Close   Gustav Mahler (1860-1911) was a Czech-Austrian composer. He studied composition and conducting at Vienna Conservatory and held important conducting positions in Leipzig, Prague, Budapest and Hamburg before, in 1897, becoming conductor and artistic director at the Vienna State Opera House. Ten years later, he left to compose and return to the concert platform. From 1908-11 he was conductor of New York Philharmonic Society. His later works consist mainly of songs and nine large-scale symphonies, five of which require voices. He is probably best known for his song-symphony *Das Lied von der Erde.* Mahler became popular in the 1980s, after the film about his life which starred Robert Powell in the title role.

Mendelssohn Grove   Felix Mendelssohn-Bartoldy (1809-47) was a German composer, son of a Hamburg banker, who was carefully nurtured as a musician and made his first public appearance as a pianist at ten years old. Mendelssohn produced quality rather than quantity, his music being tightly structured and exquisitely formed. In London, in 1829, he conducted his *Symphony in C Minor* and that summer toured Scotland, which inspired his famous *Hebrides* overture and *Scottish Symphony.* He visited England ten times and was also a brilliant pianist and organist. Mendelssohn's other popular favourites are his violin concerto of 1844 and *Midsummer Night's Dream* overture.

Moeran Close   Edward James Moeran (1894-1950) was an English composer, born in Middlesex. He studied at the Royal College of Music and, after serving in the First World War, moved to Herefordshire where he composed in various forms. Among his works are a symphony, concertos for violin, piano and 'cello and many songs.

Mozart Close   Wolfgang Amadeus Mozart (1756-91) was an Austrian composer born in Salzburg, where his house is now a tourist attraction. He was a child prodigy, playing the piano and violin by the age of four and touring Europe in concerts. He was composing by the age of five and, during his short life, his prolific output included 41 symphonies, 27 piano concertos, five violin concertos, operas such as *The Magic Flute*, chamber music, concertos for other instruments, masses and his last *Requiem*, which he feared, rightly, would be his own. After his death at 35, he was buried in an unmarked grave in the churchyard of St Mark's, Vienna, but nobody knows exactly where as 5 December 1791 was so cold that none of the few mourners followed his coffin to the burial.

Rubbra Close   Edmund Rubbra, born 1901 in Northampton, was an English composer and music critic. He took piano lessons while working as a railway clerk and in 1919 won a composition scholarship to Reading University. There he studied under Holst and Howard Jones and won a scholarship to the Royal College of Music, where he was a pupil of Vaughan-Williams. Rubbra wrote madrigals and masses and seven symphonies as well as chamber, choral and orchestral music, and songs and works for solo instruments. He was senior lecturer in music at Oxford from 1947 to 1968 and Professor of Composition at the Guildhall School of Music from 1961 to 1974. He died in 1986.

Schumann Crescent   Robert Alexander Schumann (1810-83) was a German composer and a domesticated man considered boring by his more 'romantic' contemporaries such as Wagner and Liszt. Most of his life he suffered from premonitions of madness and eventually died in a lunatic asylum in Bonn. He began his musical career as a pianist, but an accident crippled his right hand and he turned to composing piano music and writing on music. He was the best-known music critic of his day and, despite his neuroses, composed 140 songs, several symphonies and chamber music.

Strauss Grove   The famous Strauss family of Viennese dance music consisted of Johann Strauss, born 1804, and his sons Johann junior, Josef and Edward. They were all violinists, composers and conductors in turn of the family orchestra. Most of the well-known Viennese waltzes, such as *The Blue Danube* and *Tales from the Vienna Woods*, were written by Johann 'the younger', who composed over 400 waltzes as well as several operettas including *Die Fledermaus*. Richard Strauss (1864-1949) was not related to the above. He was a German composer of operas, such as *Guntram, Salome* and *Der Rosenkavalier*.

Sullivan Crescent   Sir Arthur Sullivan was born in London in 1842 and died in London in 1900. Good looking, charming and with musical talent, he was a child prodigy by the age of eight. His father was Bandmaster of the Royal Military College, Sandhurst, and Arthur learned to play every instrument in the band. He was only 13 when his anthem *Oh, Israel* was accepted for publication and a year later he was the first holder of the new Mendelssohn Scholarship at the Royal Academy of Music. In 1871 he met W.S. Gilbert and four years later their joint works began to emerge. Richard D'Oyly Carte formed a company especially for performances of their operettas: *Mikado, Pirates of Penzance, Yeoman of the Guard, Patience*, etc. Gilbert and Sullivan's relationship was often stormy, but somehow managed to survive. Arthur Sullivan was knighted in 1883.

Tallis Lane   Thomas Tallis was born about 1505 in London. He was an English musician who is regarded as 'the father of English cathedral music'. At the time of the dissolution of the monasteries, Tallis was organist at Waltham Abbey and in about 1540 he became a gentleman of the Chapel Royal. Queen Elizabeth I gave to Tallis and Byrd a monopoly of music printing. Tallis is recognised as one of the greatest contrapuntists of the English School. An adaptation of his plainsong responses and his setting of the Canticles in D minor are still in use. He wrote much church music, including a motet in 40 parts. He died at Greenwich in 1585.

Tippett Close   Sir Michael Tippett was an English composer born in London in 1905. He studied at the Royal College of Music and worked for educational organisations as a conductor from 1940-51. He first wrote chamber music and a concerto for double string orchestra, then his oratorio, *A Child of Our Time*, won him wide recognition. A pacifist, Tippett was imprisoned for three months as a conscientious objector during the Second World War. Among his works are operas, symphonies and a piano concerto. He was knighted in 1966 and died 1998.

Wagner Close   Richard Wagner (1813-83) was a German composer, controversial because of his anti-Semitic views. He composed operas, the first of which were flops, and ended up in a debtors' prison. His first success was in Paris in 1842 with *Rienzi* which he had written in prison. His well-known operas include *The Ring, The Flying Dutchman, Lohengrin, Tristan and Isolde* and *Parsifal*. Wagner's music tends to invoke either adulation or antipathy, but never indifference. He spent his life battling against debt and failure in his efforts to achieve recognition.

FOX MILNE

Sandwiched between Tongwell Street V11 grid-road and the river Ouzel, Fox Milne was the name given to the watermill in the old village of Milton Keynes in 1313 and 1418. The two roads into this commercial area are named after gem stones.

Emerald Gate   A beautiful velvety green variety of beryl, the emerald is a very valuable and highly esteemed gem stone.

Opal Drive   Usually milky white, the opal is an amorphous silica with some water content. It has a fine play of colour and some varieties are more precious than others.

GIFFARD PARK

Named after Walter Giffard, who was Lord of Longueville in Normandy and came to England with the Norman Conquest. He was a kinsman of William I and head of his army. He was given lands throughout Buckinghamshire, including the local estates of Linford, Loughton and Woolstone. His son, Walter, was the 1st Earl of Buckingham and Commissioner of the Domesday Survey of 1085/6.

THEME Recreational places in southern England

Ashdown Close   Ashdown House, Lambourn, on the Oxfordshire-Berkshire border, is owned by the National Trust. It is an extraordinary Dutch-style 17th-century house, perched on the Berkshire Downs. It is famous for its association with Elizabeth of Bohemia (the Winter Queen), Charles I's sister, to whom the house was 'consecrated'. There are spectacular views from the roof and beautiful walks through Ashdown woods.

Barbury Court   Barbury Castle Country Park is five miles south of Swindon, on the Marlborough Downs. It is a site of outstanding natural beauty, its central point being the earthworks of an Iron-Age hillfort known as Barbury Castle. Nearby are round barrows, Celtic field systems and 18th- and 19th-century flint workings. It is said that the West Saxons defeated the Britons here at the battle of Beran Byng in AD 556.

Bekonscot Court   Near Beaconsfield in Buckinghamshire, Bekonscot is probably the most famous model village in Britain and is certainly the oldest in the world. It was originally built by an accountant, Roland Callingham, as a hobby for his family and friends to enjoy. The model railway was added by his friend James Shilcock and it was opened to the public in 1929. In the 1980s a modern housing estate, model airport and intercity trains were added, but Bekonscot otherwise portrays rural England as it was in the 1930s.

Boulters Lock   Boulters Lock is on the river Thames at Maidenhead and is a well-known beauty spot. It featured in Jerome K. Jerome's *Three Men in a Boat*. It is one of the busiest stretches of the Thames and a popular riverside watering hole.

Broadway Avenue   Broadway in Worcestershire is a picturesque Cotswold village, very popular with tourists. It has thatched Cotswold stone houses and shops and Broadway Tower Country Park. The Tower is a unique historic building on top of the Cotswold ridge. It was built in the 1790s by the 6th Earl of Coventry in 35 acres of parkland and today has animal enclosures, picnic and barbecue facilities and an adventure playground, offering a complete family day out.

Bromham Mill   Bromham Mill stands by the bridge over the river Ouse at Bromham in Bedfordshire. Owned by Bedfordshire County Council, it is a working watermill where the visitor can watch flour being milled. There is also an art gallery and a picnic area.

Broxbourne Close   Broxbourne is a picturesque Hertfordshire village on the river Lee and the Lee Valley Arm of the Grand Union canal. There are scenic walks and cycle rides along the towpath and in Broxbourne woods. A boating centre offers trips with cream teas in a narrowboat, or rowing boats and motor boats may be hired. The Gunpowder Mills museum is also popular.

Cheslyn Gardens   In Staffordshire, Cheslyn Hay is a village close to Cannock Chase, an expanse of forest and heathland, threaded with miles of footpaths, where German and Commonwealth cemeteries commemorate the dead of both world wars. According to the *Oxford Dictionary of English Place-Names*, Cheslyn Hay, recorded in 1236, probably means 'coffin ridge' or 'ridge where a coffin was found'.

Clayton Gate   Clayton, on the South Downs north of Brighton, Sussex, is a village with a part-Saxon church, two 19th-century windmills called Jack and Jill and a spectacular folly, Tunnel House. This is a railwayman's cottage built in the shape of a castellated Tudor fortress, with the trains on the London-Brighton line running through the middle of it. It was built in 1841 by the London, Brighton & South Coast Railway as a home for the keeper of the Clayton tunnel.

Grafham Close   Grafham Water, Cambridgeshire is a reservoir covering six square miles and supplying towns over a 20-mile radius. It is a popular water sports amenity with sailing, boating and fishing. There is also a caravan park and extensive picnic areas and walks round the lake.

Hainault Avenue   Hainault, on the northern edge of London, used to be hunting country of heath, woodland and rich farmland. The fields and moors extended to the edge of the great Essex Forest to the north-east of London. A fragment of the forest remains at Hainault, along the Greater London boundary, and a larger portion is now known as Epping Forest.

Harlestone Court   Harlestone is a Northamptonshire village on the A428 north-west of Northampton. There is a country park with picnic areas very close to Althorp Hall, Great Brington, family home of the Spencers and last resting place of the late Diana, Princess of Wales.

Harvards Close   In the centre of Stratford-upon-Avon, Harvard House, built in 1596, was the home of Katherine Rogers, grandmother of John Harvard (1607-38), the clergyman founder of Harvard University. Now owned by the Harvard House Memorial Trust and managed by

A shared ownership property in Giffard Park. Shared ownership is an arrangement by which a purchaser can buy a percentage of the value of a private property and pay rent on the remainder.

the Shakespeare Birthplace Trust, the house is a museum of silverware and pewter.

Hodgemore Court Hodgemoor wood is a historic woodland area and Site of Special Scientific Interest lying between Seer Green and Chalfont St Giles, Buckinghamshire. It is an amenity for walkers, horse-riders and cyclists from around the area. It is owned by Buckinghamshire County Council and operated by Forest Enterprise, an agency of the Forestry Commission.

Horton Gate Horton is near Chipping Sodbury in Gloucestershire. Horton Court, owned by the National Trust, is believed to be the oldest rectory in England, but all that now remains is the 12th-century Norman great hall and a detached, late-Perpendicular ambulatory.

Kimbolton Court Kimbolton Castle, near Huntingdon, is owned by the governors of Kimbolton School. It is a late Stuart house adapted from a 13th-century fortified manor house. It was the seat of the earls and dukes of Manchester from 1615 to 1950 and is now a school. Katherine of Aragon died in the Queen's Room, which is the setting for a scene of Shakespeare's *Henry VIII*.

Knebworth Gate Knebworth House, off the A1(M) near Stevenage, Hertfordshire, has been the home of the Lytton family since 1490, and is still lived in by the Hon. Henry Lytton-Cobbold. The house was transformed in the Victorian era by Edward Bulwer-Lytton into the High Gothic fantasy it is today. It has 25 acres of gardens designed by Lutyens and Gertrude Jekyll and 250 acres of parkland with red and sika deer, a miniature railway and children's adventure playground.

Maulden Gardens Maulden Heath and Grassland at Maulden Wood, Bedfordshire is on the greensand ridge, which is a sandy scarp surrounded by the Bedfordshire and Cambridgeshire Claylands. Here are waymarked walks through Maulden Wood, the northern end of which is one of Bedfordshire's largest remnants of ancient woodland. The Grassland is a Site of Special Scientific Interest. Owned by Forest Enterprise and leased by the Greensand Trust, conifers planted in the 1980s are being removed in order to restore the site to the sheep-grazing land it once was and so encourage a diverse wildlife to return.

Oversley Court The villages of Oversley and Oversley Green on the outskirts of Alcester, Worcestershire once had a medieval manor built on the site of a Roman fort which is said to have been the precursor to the Roman town of Alcester. Close by is Ragley Hall, home of the Marquess and Marchioness of Hertford. Designed by Robert Hook in 1680, it is one of England's earliest Palladian houses.

Rainsborough Rainsborough Camp near Brackley, Northamptonshire is a Megalithic (stone) hillfort.

Rothersthorpe Rothersthorpe, Northamptonshire is just off the M1 junction

15A. The village stands near the Northampton branch of the Grand Union canal, which at this point has a flight of 13 locks, the 13th lock being a lift bridge. Rothersthorpe Country Park has picnic areas and there is an Iron-Age settlement called The Bury.

Rowsham Dell   Rousham is a peaceful, secluded manorial village by the river Cherwell near Bicester. Rousham House was built in 1635 by Sir Robert Dormer and was used as a Royalist stronghold during the Civil War. It was extended in 1738 by William Kent, who landscaped the gardens with classical temples, statues and cascades in 30 acres of woodland. Kent's mock castle gate is known as the 'Rousham Eyecatcher'. The house and gardens have been little altered since and are owned by Charles Cottrell-Dormer.

Runnymede   Runnymede, near Egham, Surrey, is a National Trust area of riverside meadows, grassland and broadleaf woodland. Part of it is a designated Site of Special Scientific Interest, owing to its rich fauna and flora. In 1215 it was the site of King John's sealing of the Magna Carta.

Salisbury Grove   Salisbury Cathedral in Wiltshire is probably the finest medieval building in Britain. It was built in one phase between 1220 and 1258 and has the highest spire and best preserved of only four surviving original examples of Magna Carta.

Shelsmore   Snelsmore Common Country Park near Newbury, Berkshire is lowland and heathland fringed by woodland.

Snowshill Court   Snowshill is a Cotswold village three miles south-west of Broadway. Snowshill Manor is a Tudor house with a 17th-century façade, owned by the National Trust. It houses a collection of craftsmanship which includes musical instruments, clocks, toys, bicycles and Japanese armour.

Wandlebury   Wandlebury Camp, Cambridgeshire is an Iron-Age fort and weekend recreation area for Cambridge on the Gog Magog Hills, which rise to only 234 feet but are the highest point in the region. In Revelation and other books of the Bible, Gog and Magog were attendant powers of Satan. In British folklore, they appear as the survivors of a race of giants destroyed by Brutus, the legendary founder of Britain. They are personified in a pair of statues in the Guildhall, London. At Wandlebury, the Roman Via Derana runs parallel to the modern main road and crosses Wort's Causeway. Wandlebury Camp was rebuilt by the British Iceni tribe

Whichford   Whichford, near Shipston-on-Stour, Warwickshire is a Cotswold village with an old stone drinking fountain on the green.

GREAT LINFORD

Great Linford was one of the 13 villages already existing in the Milton Keynes designated area. Recorded in Domesday Book in 1086 as Linforde, the name probably means 'ford where maple trees grow', derived from the Old English words hlyn (maple) and ford.

THEME **Parish History**

Alverton   Jeffrey de Alveton was rector of St Andrew's church 1332-6.

Andrewes Croft   The Reverend Henry Uthwatt Andrewes of Lathbury, near Newport Pagnell, inherited the manor of Great Linford in 1810 from his godfather and relative, Henry Uthwatt. The Uthwatt family had held the manor for the greater part of the 18th century, having inherited it from the Pritchards. Their descendants continued in ownership of the estate until it was sold to the Milton Keynes Development Corporation in about 1970.

Annes Grove   Anne Butler was the daughter of Thomas Butler, 7th Earl of Ormond, who died in August 1515. She married Sir James St Leger. Her sister, Margaret, married Sir William Boleyn and produced a son, Thomas, who became the father of Henry VIII's second wife, Anne Boleyn, to whom Anne Butler was a great-aunt. Sir Thomas Boleyn later became Earl of Wiltshire and Ormond.

Butlers Grove   Through his marriage to the daughter of John Pipard, Edmund de Boteler (the name evolved to Butler) inherited the manor of Great Linford in about 1310. Of an ancient Anglo-Irish family, and descendants of the Earls of Ormond, the Butlers remained at Great Linford until James Butler, Earl of Ormond and Earl of Wiltshire, was convicted for high treason during the Wars of the Roses. He lost his civil rights and his Wiltshire title was extinguished on 4 November 1460 by Edward IV, who granted Great Linford manor to Richard Middleton.

Campion   Richard Campion was joint lord of the manor with John Thompson after it had been granted to them by Queen Elizabeth I. The manor had been Crown property since Sir George St Leger (son of Sir James St Leger and Anne Butler) had exchanged it with Henry VIII for other lands. Campion and Thompson held it until 1632 when it was sold to Sir Robert Napier.

Church Farm Crescent   A crescent of detached houses, combining the names of Church Farm, built *c.*1650, and Crescent Farm, a Tudor manor which once operated in the area.

Church Lees   Close to the 14th-century church of St Andrew, the name means a meadow by or on church land. The field name 'Church Leas' is shown on the 1641 map of the parish, Ordnance Survey 39.

Cottisford Crescent   John Cottisford was rector of St Andrew's church 1529-34.

Deerfern Close   In the 13th century, when Ralph Pipard was lord of the manor, much of the Linford area, including Linford wood and the parkland surrounding the manor, was a deer park. Ferns, or bracken, would have grown in abundance, hence the word Deerfern, which is recorded as the name of a field.

Dovecote Croft   The Dovecote at the Old Rectory is an early 17th-century building. It has 600 nest boxes and is a scheduled monument. Dovecotes were installed at rectories or manors by the Normans to provide a food supply during the winter when meat was scarce. Some cotes housed up to 2,000 birds. Only the lord of the manor and the rector were allowed to build them, and after about 1250 most manors and rectories had a dovecote.

Fountaine Close   John Fountaine was rector of St Andrew's church from 1663 to 1677.

France Furlong   This is an ancient field name, shown on a 1641 map of Great Linford. The furlong of land was probably tenanted by the France family, who farmed at neighbouring Willen.

Gibbwin   During the reign of King John, the manor of Great Linford belonged to Geoffrey de Gibwen, one of the King's justices-itinerant. The Gibwen family founded St Andrew's church and Galfridus de Gibbewin was rector from 1215 until 1220.

Gifford Gate   Walter Giffard owned lands at Linford from the 11th century. The Giffard family were related to William the Conqueror and came to England at the time of the Norman Conquest. The first Walter Giffard was rewarded for his services with more manors than any other Norman knight and his Buckinghamshire estates take up five columns of Domesday Book. In the area now covered by Milton Keynes, he owned the Woolstones, Loughton, Bradwell, Broughton and Milton Keynes as well as Linford. After Walter Giffard III the family seems to have died out.

Granes End   Named after the field 'Granes End Furlong', possibly meaning 'the furlong at the end of the green', although a 'Greens End' is also shown on a 1641 map of Great Linford, Ordnance Survey 181.

Harpers Lane   The name is taken from a 19th-century map of Great Linford. It is the remains of an old lane across the fields now converted into a redway path.

Hartley   In the 13th century, the Pipard family kept deer on their Great Linford lands. Hartley usually means 'wood or clearing inhabited by harts or stags', from the Old English *heorot* and *leah*.

Hazelwood   Thomas de Haselwood was rector of St Andrew's church, Great Linford between 1317 and 1325. He spent many years in Newgate Prison, London, having been falsely accused by a rival of gaining the rectory by false pretences. He was cleared and released by King Edward II shortly before his death.

Heathercroft   This is possibly a modernisation of 'Hetther Long Ground', which is shown on a 1678 map of Great Linford as being a large field to the south of the village, close to Nicholas Mead.

High Street   This is the original name of the main street of the old village.

Hills Close   This is an adaptation of the field name 'Hulls Close' marked on Ordnance Survey 21, 1678 map of the area.

Kindleton   George Kindleton was rector of St Andrew's church 1661-3.

Ledbury   John Ledbury was rector of St Andrew's church 1506-17.

Linden Grove   Linden is another name for the lime tree, so probably refers to lime trees which grew here.

Lodge Gate   Indicating the gateway to Linford Lodge, which stands nearby. Also Lodge Farm is a late17th-/early 18th-century listed building.

Lower Stone Hayes and Upper Stone Hayes. These were fields, 'Stonehades', marked on a 1641 map of the area, Ordnance Survey 202. 'Hades' is said to be a dialect word for strips of land left unploughed between the cultivated areas of a field. 'Hayes' is an adaptation, although the *Oxford Dictionary of English Place-Names* suggests that the Old English word *haes* or *haese* means 'land overgrown with brushwood'.

Lufford Park   Lufford is an old variant of the name Linford.

Malins Gate   A 'furlong at Mallens Gate' was a field shown on the 1641 map of Great Linford, Ordnance Survey 166, 167, and named after John Malyn, who was a tenant of the manor in 1505-6. The Malyn family owned land and property in the parish. In the church of St Andrew there is a brass effigy to Thomas Malin, who died in 1536, and his wife, Elizabeth, who died in 1542.

Marsh Drive   The field name 'Marsh Ground' is shown on the 1678 map of the area, Ordnance Survey 105-119.

Middleton   Richard Middleton was granted the manor of Great Linford by Edward IV. He only held it for a short time before it reverted to the Crown and in 1467 it was granted to Princess Elizabeth of York, who became the queen of Henry VII. Henry Middleton was rector of St Andrew's church from 1469 to 1491.

Mill Hayes   Taken from the field name listed as 'Furlong between Windmill Hades' (Ordnance Survey 123), next to 'Windmill Hill' marked on the 1641 map. A windmill was built at Great Linford in the second half of the 13th century.

Newmans Close   This was the name of a field marked on the 1678 map of Great Linford lying just south of the village. There were several families called Newman, probably all related, and farming all over the Milton Keynes area.

Nicholas Mead   This was the ancient name of a large field on the east side of Great Linford and bordering Penny Land field, shown on a 1678 map of Great Linford. The Mead is a listed late 17th-century house. There are a number of gravestones in the churchyard belonging to members of the Mead family.

Paddock Close   Leads to the paddocks of Linford Lodge, many of which have now been built upon.

Parklands   Adjacent to the grounds of Linford Manor, the name refers to the lands of Manor Park, to which the road leads.

Pipard   The Pipard family held the manor of Great Linford some time during the late 12th and/or early 13th centuries, after the de Gibwen family and before the Botelers (Butlers). Ralph Pipard was created a Baron by Edward I on 26 January 1297 and the title expired with him in 1302.

St Leger Court   Named after the St Leger family who held the manor in the 15th century.

St Leger Drive   Thomas St Leger was rector of St Andrew's church, Great Linford in 1527-8. The St Leger family held the manor in the late 15th and early 16th centuries, having apparently had it passed to them by Elizabeth of York, second wife of Henry VII. Sir George St Leger is believed to have exchanged it with Henry VIII for other lands.

Railway Walk, Great Linford, where the old railway track used to be, with the station platform on the right.

Beside the Grand Union canal at Linford Wharf, this was the Old Wharf Inn *until the 1970s. It is now a private house.*

Restored brick kilns at Great Linford.

Sandy Close   Richard Sandy (alias Napier) was rector of St Andrew's church 1589-1634. The son of Sir Richard Napier of Luton Hoo, he studied physics and astrology under Dr Simon Forman, notorious in his day as a quack doctor. The experience had a life-long influence on Sandy, who also posed as a physician. Claiming to be in conversation with the Angel Raphael, who predicted whether his patients would recover or die, he achieved a creditable reputation, especially among the gentry.

In 1629 the Earl of Sunderland spent several months as a patient at Sandy's house in Great Linford. It was said that the rector was so devout his knees grew horny from all the praying. He died while at prayer on 15 April 1634, and is buried in the churchyard.

Solar Court   So named when eight low-energy, solar-powered houses here were the subject of a study of energy flows carried out by Milton Keynes Development Corporation following the oil crisis of the early 1970s.

Station Terrace   The row of cottages which make up Station Terrace flank the old Great Linford railway station and back on to what was once the branch line running between Wolverton and Newport Pagnell. The line was opened in 1865 to carry goods and from 1867 carried passengers as well. It closed to passengers on 5 September 1964, but carried goods until 1967 when it was closed down and the track taken up. Milton Keynes Development Corporation laid a redway, now called Railway Walk, which follows the route of the old railway line. The station platform still remains.

Summer Hayes   The exact origin is not known, but most likely is the name of a field.

The Crescent   A crescent-shaped group of houses.

The Wharf   The wharf beside the Grand Union canal at Great Linford was established soon after the canal was built in the early 19th century. It was used to load bricks made in the brick kilns at Great Linford on to horse-drawn narrowboats, and was also a commercial link between Leicestershire and Bedfordshire. Joseph Coleman, a Bedford grocer, had bulk supplies of Leicester cheeses delivered by canal to Linford wharf from where it was collected and taken by wagon to Bedford. The *Old Wharf Inn*, a listed 19th-century building, was a pub until the early 1970s.

Well Hayes   Taken from the field name 'Fullwell Hades' shown on the 1641 map, Ordnance Survey 130.

Willen Lane   This is a stretch of the old lane which once led to Willen.

Woad Lane   Linford and Newport Pagnell were main areas locally for the growth and preparation of woad for the dyeing industry. The 1821 census records four families still cultivating woad and living in turf huts. Woad is a plant, the leaves of which exude a permanent blue dye.

Wood Lane   Originally part of the lane leading to Linford Wood. Wood House stands beside Linford Lodge. This former country lane tails off into a redway path.

KENTS HILL

Kents Hill was the name of a field shown on a map of Milton Keynes dated 1685 and Ordnance Survey map numbers 6, 7 and 21. In Tudor times, the dukes of Kent held about 20 manors in this area, after Edmund, Baron Grey, lord of the manors of Bletchley, Simpson and Great Brickhill and a Yorkist during the Wars of the Roses, had been rewarded by Edward IV with the title of Earl of Kent in 1465. There was also a tenant farmer, James Kent, who in 1789 held fields in the Kents Hill area.

THEME **The County of Kent. Since these streets were named in the early 1970s, the boundaries of Kent have been altered; therefore some of these places are now in Sussex.**

Badgers Oak   Badgers Oaks, in the parish of Cranbrook, is shown on OS map of Kent number 244. There is also a private house called Badgers' Oak at Badgers Mount, to the south-east of Bromley in Kent, and Badgers' Oak Veterinary Surgery on the Hastings Road near Northiam, East Sussex.

Baynham Mead   This must surely refer to Bayham Abbey near Lamberhurst on the Kent-Sussex border. Spread out in the peaceful setting of the wooded valley of the river Teise are the ruins of the Premonstratensian monastery founded in about 1208 by Robert Thornham. The church, the abbey buildings and 14th-century gatehouse are among the remaining buildings of what was once a religious house of White Canons, as the Premonstratensians became known. After its suppression in 1525, Henry VIII leased the abbey to a succession of noblemen.

Bedgebury Place Bedgebury Manor and estate dates back to at least AD 815 and was owned by the Bedgebury family until about 1450, when it passed to the Culpeppers and then to Sir James Hayes who built the present manor house, which is now a girls' school. The estate included Bedgebury Forest which is now the National Pinetum and Forest Gardens. Established in 1925 as the National Conifer Collection, it was developed jointly by the Forestry Commission and the Royal Botanic Gardens at Kew. The Pinetum now has 6,241 tree specimens, 2,100 of which are species of conifer and cultivars and some of which are either extinct in 'the wild' or extremely rare. Lying off the B2079 from Goudhurst, Bedgebury Forest covers 2,600 acres which surround 320 acres of parkland.

Birdlip Lane This lane links Kents Hill to Walnut Tree and is named after the turnpike at Birdlip in Gloucestershire.

Copthorne Place In West Sussex between East Grinstead and Crawley, Copthorne is a village off the M23 near Gatwick Airport. It has a population of 7,000 and supports 200 small businesses and the *Copthorne Hotel*, where many of the villagers work. Its Victorian church of St John the Evangelist, built in 1877, was the scene of the wedding of Fatima Whitbread and Andrew Norman, the sports promoter, in May 1997 and their son, Ryan, was baptised there two years later. Many sports personalities attended the wedding at which Jonathan Edwards read from the Bible. Norman Wisdom's daughter, Jacqueline, lived in Copthorne and, given away by her father, was married there in 1982. The late Richard Dimbleby was also married there in 1936 as his sister-in-law was churchwarden at the time.

Crowborough Lane On the A26 Tunbridge Wells to Lewes road, Crowborough, once an area of heathland, was developed in Victorian times as a resort on the edge of Ashdown Forest. From 1909 Sir Arthur Conan Doyle lived in Crowborough and built Windelsham Manor where he wrote many of his *Sherlock Holmes* stories. After his death in 1930 he was buried in the garden but, five years later, his widow had his remains removed to the family vault.

Eridge Green Eridge Green is a small village on the Crowborough to Tunbridge Wells road. In 1202 it was known as Ernerigg, which means a ridge frequented by eagles. The village pub, the *Nevill Crest and Gun*, takes its name from the Nevill family, Earls of Abergavenny, who have held the estates of Eridge Park since the Norman Conquest. During the 16th century the Nevills financed the making of guns at the village forge and in 1792 the Earl of Abergavenny remodelled the house in the park and renamed it Eridge Castle. It was demolished before the Second World War, and a modern house built in its place reverted to the name Eridge Park. The estate provided employment for the people of Eridge Green well into the 20th century.

Felbridge   Lying on the Kent-Surrey-Sussex borders and two miles north of East Grinstead, Felbridge was once on the main stage-coach route from London to Brighton. A number of fine old farms, cottages and other historic buildings remain, although others were demolished in 1963 to make way for light industrial development, and Felbridge Place, which was built in 1763, was pulled down in 1972 to make way for Whittington College.

Fordcombe Lea   A small village in the Weald of Kent, in the valleys of the rivers Medway and Eden. It has a church, a primary school with only 103 pupils, a village green and a cricket team. Within a two-mile radius of the village are Groombridge Place gardens and enchanted forest, and two medieval castles: Penshurst Place, ancestral home of the Sidney family since 1552, is owned by Philip Sidney, Viscount De L'Isle; Hever Castle dates from the 13th century and was the seat of the Boleyn family.

Frithwood Crescent   Frith Wood is shown on an old Ordnance Survey map, number 131, of Hadlow parish, Kent, and Frith Wood Farm and woodland are shown on OS number 244 in the parish of Hawkhurst. Frithwood means an area of sparse brushwood and is possibly used here as a derivation of Thistley Field, which was the name of a large field shown on a map of Kents Hill in 1782 as covering the land where Frithwood Crescent now stands. By the early 20th century the field had become known as Thrifty field.

Goudhurst Court   Goudhurst, on the A262 nine miles east of Tunbridge Wells, has typical Kentish weather-board and tile-hung houses flanking its High Street and around the village pond. The Culpepper family has many memorials in the 15th-century village church of St Mary. Sir Thomas Culpepper, known as the Iron Master, owned an iron foundry at the manor of Bedgebury where were cast guns, some of which were used in the fleet that fought the Spanish Armada in 1588.

Groombridge   The village of Groombridge lies off the A264, four miles south-west of Tunbridge Wells and is renowned for the Groombridge Gang of smugglers which was formed in 1733 and worked in league with the Hawkhurst Gang. Groombridge Place is a 17th-century moated manor standing in 200 acres of award-winning gardens which include rose gardens, a secret garden, a 'drunken' topiary and an enchanted forest of ancient woodland.

Hartfield Close   On the north edge of Ashdown Forest, Hartfield was probably named after the proliferation of hart deer roaming the forest which was once a royal deer park. Once an agricultural village, Hartfield became a centre for iron and timber and had a furnace and a forge. In

1905 the Milne family bought Cotchford Farm, where A.A. Milne wrote his *Winnie the Pooh* stories using the area around the farm as his settings. The bridge over a stream on the farm is where poohsticks were invented, and in the 1920s Christopher Robin Milne could be seen visiting the village shops with his nanny.

High Halden   The village of High Halden lies between the Weald of Kent and Romney Marsh, on the edge of the old Wealden forest. Tiffenden Manor, south of the village green, is said to have been farmed for 1,000 years. Today the village appears to have more new than old houses.

Hoathly Mews   About 15 miles apart as the crow flies, there is East Hoathly in East Sussex, off the A22 Uckfield to Eastbourne road, and West Hoathly in West Sussex, to the south-east of Crawley. The old houses and cottages of West Hoathly are perched 600 feet up on a ridge in the High Weald. In a country cottage garden, the 15th-century, timber-framed Priest House is now a museum, the old church has recently been restored and the Tudor manor house is now a hotel. East Hoathly once had a thriving trug-making industry and the busy A22 running through it, but is now a quiet, picturesque village with a 13th-century pub at its centre and several listed buildings.

Knox Bridge   Knox Bridge is a small village on the A229 at the north side of Cranbrook Common.

Lamberhurst Grove   Lamberhurst, about ten miles east of Tunbridge Wells on the A21, was once the centre of the Wealdon iron industry and was a coaching stop on the London to Hastings route. The ruins of the original 14th-century moated Scotney Castle and the 19th-century 'new' Scotney Castle stand in beautiful gardens on the south-east side of the village. On the west side is a 16th-century, half-timbered and tile-hung building called The Owl House because of its historical involvement with wool smugglers, known as 'owlers' because they operated at night.

Millbank Place   Mill Bank, in the parish of Hoath, is shown on a 1905 revised Ordnance Survey map of Kent number 112, and Mill Bank Place is shown as being a nursery near Ashford.

Pipston Green   This is possibly a corruption of Pipsden, near Hawkhurst, shown on 1905 revised Ordnance Survey map 267.

Pondgate   This most probably refers to Poundgate, East Sussex, which is a small village on the A26 between Crowborough Common and Newnham Park Wood. However, there are two Pond Farms and five Pond Woods marked on old maps of several Kent parishes.

Rolvenden Grove   Rolvenden is a small but busy village on a hill on the A28 about four miles from Tenterden in Kent. In its wide high street can be found the C.M. Booth Motor Museum which has a collection of Morgan three-wheelers, vintage cars, motorbikes and toy and model cars. Great

Maytham Hall, designed by Lutyens in 1910, stands in 18 acres with a walled garden which was the inspiration for *The Secret Garden* by Frances Hodson Burnett. The Hall is now apartments for active retired people.

Shernfold   Shernfold Park appears to be the name of a business park in the Frant and Tunbridge Wells area of Kent.

Shirley Moor   This is an area of moorland to the south-east of Tenterden in Kent.

Smarden Bell   Smarden Bell and Smarden, north of Tenterden off the A274, are picturesque Wealden wool villages of white, weather-boarded houses. Next to the village pump in Smarden, the Dragon House was built in 1331 for a family of Dutch weavers brought over by Edward III to weave broadcloth. Still standing today is a cloth hall, dated about 1420, with the hoist used for lifting bales of cloth to the loft still hanging from a gable. Smarden was a weaving town until the 19th century, after which hop-growing was introduced to which oast houses in the village bear witness.

Southbridge Grove   The only Southbridge found is in the Croydon area of Surrey, where Southbridge Road joins the Old Roman Way down to Kent.

Speldhurst Court   Speldhurst is an old Kent village dating back to at least the eighth century. The *George and Dragon* inn was originally built in 1212 and the 13th-century church was destroyed, apart from the tower, when it was hit by a bolt of lightning in 1791. It was rebuilt in 1870. During the 20th century, Speldhurst expanded as a dormitory village for Tunbridge Wells, but has retained its very pretty village centre.

Sweetlands Corner   Is on the A229 north of Knox Bridge near Staplehurst.

Tenterden Crescent   Tenterden is an attractive town on the edge of the Weald of Kent and close to Romney Marsh. A wool-trading centre in the 15th century, it is believed to have been the birthplace in 1472 of William Caxton, the father of English printing. The town has a wide main street with many fine 18th-century houses and, at Small Hythe Place, there is a museum dedicated to the memory of the actress Dame Ellen Terry.

Ticehurst Close   Ticehurst lies on the B2099 a few miles south-east of Wadhurst, East Sussex. The village has several old manors including the moated Pashley Manor built in 1292 by the Passole family. It has connections with the Boleyn family and is open to the public. There are shops in the village centre and a church with memorials recording the past life of the village.

Tudeley Hale   Tudeley, near Tonbridge on the A21, is close to Tudeley Woods RSPB nature reserve. All Saints' church, built in the 18th century on Saxon foundations, is famous for its stained-glass windows designed by the Russian artist, Marc Chagall. Installed in 1966 when the church was restored, they were commissioned by Sir Henry and Lady d'Avigdor-Goldsmid of Tonbridge as a memorial to their daughter, Sarah, who was drowned in a sailing accident in 1963.

Tunbridge Grove Whether Tonbridge or Tunbridge Wells was intended here is unclear. Nevertheless, before the 19th century, Tonbridge was a very large parish which included Tunbridge Wells until it became a separate parish in 1833. Only a few miles apart in central, scenic Kent, Tonbridge lies on the river Medway, while Tunbridge Wells is in the valley of the river Tiese. Tonbridge is famed for its public school founded in 1533 by a former Mayor of London, Sir Andrew Judde, who was a member of the Worshipful Company of Skinners. In about 1606 the health-giving properties of the spring at Tunbridge Wells were discovered and the town developed as a spa resort, popular with royalty. Charles I's queen, Henrietta Maria, often visited and the 17th-century church has an unusual dedication to King Charles the Martyr. Queen Victoria also visited and Edward VII granted it the status of 'Royal' Tunbridge Wells in 1909.

Wadhurst Lane Wadhurst, which lies about six miles south-east of Tunbridge Wells, has a long High Street flanked by tile-hung cottages and was once a thriving hub of the Wealden iron industry. The church of St Peter and St Paul has 30 iron slab memorials dating between 1617 and 1790, many of which commemorate the local iron-master family of Barhams. On 8 December 1863 the last bare-fisted prize-fight in England took place at Wadhurst.

Wilsley Pound Wilsley Pound is a small village on the A262 on the edge of Cranbrook Common. The area was probably once used as a pound, or enclosure, for animals.

KENTS HILL PARK

This area of Kents Hill contains the local park and playing fields, an area of woodland, the British Telecommunications Training College, a conference hotel and the campus of what was originally de Montfort University until it closed down in early 2003. The buildings are now an additional part of the Open University.

Durgate Durgate Wood is shown on the 1905 revised Ordnance Survey map number 228 as being in the parish of Lyminge. Confusingly, about 20 miles northwards, Dargate is one of a chain of small, pretty villages beside the A299 which runs from the end of the M2 to the coast at Whitstable. In wooded countryside, the creeper-clad *Dove* public house stands in Plum Pudding Lane and serves the local beer of the Shepherd Neame brewery, Britain's oldest, based at Faversham, since 1573.

Hammerwood Gate Hammerwood Park near East Grinstead in Sussex is a country mansion built in 1792 as an Apollo's hunting lodge by Benjamin Latrobe, architect of the White House and the Capitol in Washington DC. In the 1970s it was owned by the rock band Led Zepplin and in 1982 was rescued from dereliction. Now owned by David Pinnegar and his family, the house is open to the public during the summer months.

Hawkhurst Gate   Hawkhurst lies on the A268 near its junction with the A229. The largest village in this region of Kent, the old part, known as the Moor, clusters around the 12th-century church while the newer part has 18th-century weather-boarded houses and shops. Historically it is famous for the Hawkhurst Gang, ruthless smugglers who operated between 1735 and 1750. Their range covered the coastline from Kent to Dorset and they could muster 500 men when needed for a major smuggle. Their main meeting place was the *Oak and Ivy Inn* until their leaders were caught and executed in 1748-9.

Timbold Drive   Timbold Hill is shown on the 1905 revised Ordnance Survey map 267, in the parish of Lenham.

KINGSTON

Just north of Wavendon on the road once known as the King's Highway, the Kingston bridge crosses the Broughton Brook on the A5130 near Fen Farm. The fields on which this shopping and industrial centre stands were known as Kingsoe Leys, as shown on Ordnance Survey 41, a 1685 map of the old Milton Keynes parish.

THEME **Locations associated with English Kings**

Chippenham Drive   In Wiltshire, Chippenham was founded around AD 600 as a village in the Saxon kingdom of Wessex and was a royal property of the king. King Alfred the Great is said to have had a residence there. Grown into a town by 1066, it lost its royal prestige under the Normans.

Greyfriars Court   In the churchyard of Greyfriars church in Edinburgh in 1638, the first signatures were placed on the National Covenant, a sacred promise to resist the 'corruptions' of the Anglican faith forced upon Scotland by Charles I.

Lasborough Road   At the battle of Worcester on 3 September 1651, King Charles II (in exile in Scotland) commanded the Royalist forces in what was to be a last-ditch attempt against Cromwell's Parliamentarians. Outnumbered two-to-one, the Royalists fought valiantly for three hours before being defeated. The King managed to escape capture and fled to Lasborough near Dursley in Gloucestershire. From there he roamed England for six weeks before finding a boat to take him to France.

Maidstone Road   The county town of Kent, Maidstone was the capital of the Saxon kingdom of West Kent. The town has a 14th-century Archbishops Palace which was the residence of the Archbishops of Canterbury until 1538. It was also the site of several rebellions: Wat Tyler's Peasants' Revolt in 1381, the Kentish Rebellion led by Jack Cade in 1450 and a revolt instigated by Sir Thomas Wyatt against Queen Mary Tudor in 1554. During the English Civil War, Fairfax destroyed the Royalist forces at Maidstone.

Mandeville Drive   Lord Viscount Mandeville, who became Duke of Manchester, was a Parliamentarian during the English Civil Wars and commanded the Eastern Association in 1643. He was one of a few peers who fought against the King. Almost 500 years earlier, in about 1130, Geoffrey de Mandeville, Earl of Essex was Constable of the Tower and turned traitor, first to King Stephen and then to Empress Matilda. He became an outlaw and was attacked and killed in the Cambridgeshire fens in 1144.

Newmarket Court. Racing, 'the sport of kings', was established at Newmarket by James I. It became the headquarters of horse racing in the 17th century and has been the home of the Jockey Club since it was formed in 1772.

Whitehall Avenue   A street in London named after the royal palace of Whitehall which was built for James I. Charles I was executed here before it was destroyed by fire in 1698. The Banqueting House, designed by Inigo Jones in 1622 with ceilings by Rubens, was all that survived the fire. The street, Whitehall, became the place of government offices after George II offered 10 Downing Street to Robert Walpole.

Winchester Circle   Winchester in Hampshire was the capital of Saxon Wessex and residence of Saxon kings. It was also the capital of Norman kings until they moved their capital to London, although Parliament continued to meet at Winchester until 1485. Henry VII's first son was baptised in the cathedral.

MILTON KEYNES AND MIDDLETON

Milton Keynes is the ancient and once agricultural village which gave its name to the new city. One of several options, it was favoured by Lord Campbell of Eskan, first Chairman of the Development Corporation, because it combined the name of his favourite poet, John Milton, with that of his most admired economist, John Maynard Keynes. The name Milton Keynes actually derives from the Anglo-Saxon 'Middel-tun' and the Old French 'Cahaignes' family, who owned the manor between about 1165 and 1288. Although the original village retains the name of Milton Keynes, the new development which now surrounds it is called Middleton. Several listed 17th-century white-painted, thatched cottages remain at the core of the village.

THEME Milton Keynes Parish History

Babington Close   Adam Babynton was rector of All Saints' church, Milton Keynes from 1423 until his death in 1427. He was buried in the chancel and a brass effigy of him can be seen in the church. Dr Francis Babington was rector 1559-65, during which time he was also Master of Balliol College, Oxford, rector of Lincoln College and adviser to the Earl of Leicester until 1563. Believed to be a Roman Catholic sympathiser, he resigned his Milton Keynes living in 1565 and went abroad, where he died in 1569.

Bereville Court   The de Berevilles held a manor in Milton Keynes at some time during the 12th century.

Bowling Leys   On a land survey of 1789, Bowling Leys is shown as three small tenements with gardens tenanted by James Page. A close adjoining Bowling Leys was upland meadow. A leys, or leas, could be either arable land, a meadow, or land left fallow.

Broughton Road   This is a section of the old road which ran between the villages of Milton Keynes and Broughton.

Campania Close   Anciently, there were at least three manors in the area covered by Milton Keynes parish, one of which was in the possession of the Campania family. Peter de Campania was in possession of it in 1294. William de Campania, who was connected with Snelshall Priory in 1225, may well have been a member of the same family.

Clare Croft   The Clare family anciently owned a manor at the neighbouring village of Little Woolstone. More recently, another Clare family lived in Milton Keynes and their graves in All Saints' churchyard date from 1829 to 1949.

Claridge Drive   The Claridge family were living in the village during the 19th century and into the 1950s. Their graves in All Saints' churchyard cover the period 1885 to 1952 and they were probably farmers, for Rosetta Claridge, who died in 1885, moved to Milton Keynes from Colesdale Farm, Northaw, Bedfordshire.

Coin Close   It is possible that Corn, not Coin, Close was the name intended here. In this area of the parish in 1685, Corn Close was a 29-acre field which, by 1838, had been divided into upper and lower Corn Close, as shown on maps and surveys of those dates.

Dalton Gate   John Neale Dalton was rector of All Saints' church, Milton

The Swan Inn, *Milton Keynes Village on fire in 1970 and (right) as it is today.*

Keynes 1857-80. He founded the village school and is buried in the churchyard. Another John Dalton was rector from 1427-39.

Deacon Place   In All Saints' church there are monumental inscriptions to Harriet Deacon, who died in 1900 aged 78 years, and William Deacon, who died in August 1906. Both are buried in the churchyard.

Digby Croft   The Digby family became prominent in north Buckinghamshire after Sir Everard Digby of Gunpowder Plot fame married Maria Moulso of Gayhurst Manor, near Newport Pagnell. They had two sons, John and Kenelm. John became a Royalist Major General in the Civil War and no record has been found of his having married. Sir Kenelm's marriage to Venetia Stanley produced five children, of whom one, John Digby, born in 1627, married Margaret Longueville. She was the daughter of Sir Edward Longueville, lord of the manors of Wolverton and Woughton-on-the-Green until he sold both manors to the Trustees of Dr Radcliffe's estate in about 1712. There was also a Thomas Digby who, in about 1555, contended the leasehold of the manor of Milton Keynes, Digby claiming that the lease had been assigned to him by Richard Woodall and not transferred to Woodall's son, Thomas. Who won the argument is unclear, but the manor was repossessed by the freeholder, Sir Humphrey Stafford, in 1563.

Dormans Close   The Dorman family owned land in this area during the 16th century.

Finch Close   The noble Finch family owned the manor of Milton Keynes for nearly 300 years from 1667 to 1939 and were major landowners. Heneage Finch,1st Earl of Nottingham, was Solicitor-General at the Restoration and took part in the trial of the regicides. He became Attorney-General in 1670, Lord Chancellor in 1674 and presided at the trial of Stafford in 1680. His son, Daniel, was a statesman who in 1729 added the title 6th Earl of Winchelsea to that of 2nd Earl of Nottingham. The last Finch in the village was Wilfred

Henry, who served as a Lieutenant in the Royal Engineers and died, aged 56, in 1939. The estate passed to a distant cousin.

Great Linch   Great Linch was pastureland of 28 acres in the west of the parish, tenanted in 1789 by the widow Fountain. A 'linch' was a boundary ridge, a terrace or ledge, or an unploughed strip of land.

Griffith Gate   This possibly refers to John Griffith of nearby Moulsoe who is listed as a freeholder on the 1784 Poll for Buckingham. He held land in Loughton and Broughton, which abuts Milton Keynes parish.

Halswell Place   The *Victoria County History for Buckinghamshire* records a Nicholas Halswell as being in possession of a share in a cottage near All Saints' church in 1565.

Heneage Finch, 1st Earl of Nottingham, 17th-century lord of the manor of Milton Keynes.

Hensman Gate   A Hensman family lived in the village in the early 20th century. William died in 1954, Ena in 1975 and both are buried in the churchyard. In 1685 there was a six-acre field known as Hencemans Little Close located to the west of Hensman Gate.

Hillbeck Grove   According to the *Victoria County History for Buckinghamshire*, Robert Halebot, or Hillbeck, married Maud, daughter of John de Bereville, in the early 13th century. In 1227, she claimed some land in Milton Keynes.

Hopkins Close   Lesser or Hopkins Marsh was a 17-acre field, shown on a survey of Milton Keynes parish lands in 1685.

Howe Court   William Howe was a tenant farmer in the late 18th and early 19th centuries. He held a house and garden with a yard, outbuildings and an orchard and several acres of pasture on which he grazed cattle.

Kingsoe Leys   The old name 'Kingsoe Fenn' refers to the flat, marshy area towards Kingston, also anciently known as Kingsoe Leys, shown on a survey of 1685 as covering 37 acres. On the 1789 land survey it is described as arable land containing a barn and a rickyard, with Kingsoe meadow, all of which was farmed by Mrs Ann West.

Lady Meadow Court   Lady Meadow was an 11-acre field shown on the map and survey of 1789 as tenanted by the widow Head and her son, John Head, who were major farmers in Milton Keynes parish.

Little Hame   Little Hame was the name of a field, shown on the 1789 land survey as being a 13-acre meadow tenanted by Thomas Abbot. By 1883 it was tenanted by John Clode. *Hame* is another word for home.

Luke Place   Luke de Keynes held the manor of Milton Keynes until his death in 1262.

Manor Close   Referring to the manor which, since Domesday, has passed from the de Cahaignes (later Keynes) family successively to the Aylesburys, Staffords and Finches, who retained the manor from 1667 to 1939. William de Keynes was the man who captured King Stephen at Lincoln. Manor Farm House, a listed late 17th- to early 18th-century building, still survives.

Meadow Lane   There were several meadows in old Milton Keynes, such as March meadow and Rough meadow, shown on a 1789 land survey as being roughly in this area of the parish. In 1838 there was also a tenant farmer named Andrew Meadows.

Merchant Place   In 1946, the Milton Keynes manorial estate was sold to the Society of Merchant Venturers of Bristol, who held it in trust until it was purchased from them by the Milton Keynes Development Corporation. Dating back to the 14th century, the Merchant Venturers originally opened up sea trade routes, forming themselves into a guild in order to protect their interests and to obtain control of the shipping entering and leaving the port of Bristol.

Noon Layer Drive   Noon Layer hill was an upland meadow at the north-eastern tip of Milton Keynes parish, where the fire station now stands. Shown on a land survey of 1685, and on subsequent maps and surveys, it covered 12 acres and in 1789 was tenanted by Mrs Ann West. The meaning is obscure, but it is tempting to think that a noon layer was a hen which layed its eggs at noon.

Norman Crescent   This road was probably named after Anthony Norman, who was rector of Holy Trinity church, Great Woolstone in 1720-1.

Parneleys   This was the name of a house which once stood on this site and is shown on a 1585 map of the area.

Parrock Lane   Parrock is an old word for a small enclosure or paddock and derives from the Old English *pearroc*.

Powell Haven   William Powell was rector of All Saints' church, Milton Keynes, 1522-9. Also, the Powell family were tenant farmers of Southside Farm during the early 20th century, until after the Second World War.

Savage Croft   William Savage is shown on the land surveys of 1789 and 1838 as being a tenant at will of a house and garden near the village centre.

Cottages at Milton Keynes Village.

Simms Croft Mr John Simms is shown on both land surveys of 1789 and 1838 as the tenant of a farmyard, a barn and part of Fountain's yard. Also in 1789 there was a Hugh Sims who, with Richard Brittain and the widow Green (all paupers), rented three small tenements of a house and garden.

Southside Lane On the south side of Milton Keynes village, Southside Farm was the largest of the four main farms and held the most land. The large farmhouse was built in the early 19th century and is a listed building. It remained a working farm through the Second World War when it was tenanted by the Powell family.

Swayne Rise A Philip Swayne is recorded as living in the parish of Milton Keynes in the late 16th century. A document dated October 1594 reveals that he was ordered to pay eight shillings' tax on goods valued at £300.

Wadworth Holme Wadworths Upper and Lower Holme pastures were five- and six-acre fields farmed in 1838 by George Payne. The previous tenant farmer in 1789 was Robert Holme. Richard Wadsworth was rector of Holy Trinity church, Little Woolstone, from 1765-80.

Walton Road This is a section of the old road leading from Milton Keynes to Walton.

Webbs Home Close Webbs Home Close was the name of a field tenanted by James Page in 1789. Presumably, the Webbs were farming the area at an earlier time.

Willen Road This is a section of the old country lane which once led to Willen.

Wingfield Grove   The Honourable Wingfield Stratford Twistleton Wykeham Fiennes, MA, was rector of All Saints' church, Milton Keynes 1880-1910.

Wolston Meadow   Wolston was an alternative spelling of Woolstone. The land survey of 1789 shows Woolston Great Meadow, a 12-acre field and Woolston Little Meadow, six acres, tenanted by William Pancoust.

Worrelle Avenue   The name of Robert Worrelle, of the parish of Milton Keynes, is listed in a 1594 document under the title Subsidiary Assessment, showing details of 'value' (£3 in goods) and 'tax' (8s.)

The Honourable Wingfield Stratford Twistleton Wykeham Fiennes, MA, rector of All Saints' church, 1880-1910.

Wrens Park   Wrens Park was a pasture of eight acres, tenanted in 1789 by Mrs Head, a widow, and her son John. The Heads were major tenant farmers with a farmhouse and nearly 280 acres of land. By 1838, George Payne had taken over Wrens Park.

MONKSTON

Monkston derives from Monxton's Bridge, which was an ancient bridge over the Ouzel river on the Milton Keynes-Woughton parish boundary.

THEME **The theme originally chosen by Milton Keynes Development Corporation for Monkston roads was Bird and Wildlife Sanctuaries. This appears to have been exchanged for Medieval Monasteries, which was originally intended for Tattenhoe. However, some of these monastic sites are also bird or wildlife sanctuaries.**

Abbeydore Grove   The remains of a Cistercian abbey church, founded in the 12th century, are still in use as the local parish church in the village of Abbey Dore, situated nine miles south-west of Hereford. The church today is only a small part of the original building, which underwent many changes and a great deal of restoration before, during and after the dissolution and as late as the close of the 19th century. This 'abbey by the stream' – *dour* being roughly translated from the Welsh word for water – was converted to a parish church in the mid-17th century.

Ampleforth   In North Yorkshire, Ampleforth today is home to a Catholic monastery and college which plays a large part in the life of the local community. Ampleforth Abbey was founded in 1608 for Benedictine monks and was dedicated to St Lawrence the Martyr. After the dissolution of the monasteries by Henry VIII, his daughter, Queen Mary Tudor, revived the Catholic faith and monastic life at Ampleforth began with a few exiled English Catholics. Over the next 185 years, men were trained for the English mission.

Aylesford Grove   The Carmelite priory, also known as The Friars, which was founded in the mid-13th century, annually attracts many thousands of visitors to its site by the river Medway at Aylesford in Kent. What they see today is a restoration of the site and of the main building which, in the late 17th century, was converted into a mansion house, which is how it remained until 1930 when it was severely damaged by fire. The Carmelites once again became the owners of the medieval home and a programme of restoration and redevelopment over a decade from the mid-1960s has resulted in a modern working priory and a thriving pilgrimage centre.

Balmerino Close   Situated opposite Dundee overlooking the Firth of Tay, Balmerino, a Cistercian abbey, was founded in about 1230 by Queen Ermengarde, the great granddaughter of William the Conqueror. By the mid-16th century it had become one of the richest abbeys in Scotland and, in 1565, numbered Mary Queen of Scots among its visitors. Today the site is managed by the National Trust of Scotland and can be visited by the public.

Bardsey Court   A community established in AD 430 on the one-and-a-half mile long, half-mile wide island of Bardsey off the coast of the Lleyn Peninsula in North Wales, is believed to be the first monastic settlement in Britain. It was one of the most important places of pilgrimage in the Middle Ages, and its remoteness made it an ideal place of refuge. In the 12th century an Augustinian abbey (St Mary) was built. Only a small community now lives on the island all the year round, joined in the summer by those on organised retreats and others who recognise Bardsey as an important site for migrant birds.

Blanchland Circle   Blanchland village, in a glen on the Derwent river in Northumberland, dates back to 1165, when Walter de Bolbec founded a Premonstratensian monastery here. This was an order of Canons Regular, founded in 1119 by St Norbert and otherwise known as Norbertines, or White Canons. After the Reformation, the monastic estate fell into decline, but was bought in 1623 by the Forster family of Bamburgh. In 1699 Dorothy Forster married the Bishop of Durham, Lord Crewe, who bought the debt-ridden estate in 1704.

Boxgrove Court   The Benedictine priory at Boxgrove, near Chichester, West Sussex, was one of many that suffered at the dissolution. Work had begun on the site in the early 1100s, but several buildings were destroyed on the orders of Henry VIII in the 16th century. The remaining part of the priory church today remains in use as the parish church. Other parts have survived, including a pillar and several arches.

Brecon Court   A priory was established at Brecon, in what is today the Brecon Beacons National Park, by monks of the Benedictine order in the early years of the 12th century. It was closed at the dissolution in 1537, when ownership of the monastic buildings passed to a local man. The church became Brecon's parish church until the disestablishment of the church in Wales in 1920, when the priory church became the cathedral church of the new diocese of Swansea and Brecon. It was later altered, with buildings in the Close being used as vestries and accommodation for clergy.

Bridlington Crescent   Walter de Gaunt founded Bridlington Priory, Yorkshire in about 1072. In 1113 Henry I granted a charter to the Canons Regular of St Augustine and the priory grew rapidly in wealth, property and power. One of its 15th-century canons, George Ripley, was a well-known philosopher and alchemist. During the Reformation, Prior William Woode played an active part in the Yorkshire insurrection known as the Pilgrimage of Grace, after which he was arrested, tried and executed in 1538. The priory church containing the original nave stands today, but the conventual buildings which once surrounded it were destroyed, decayed and eventually disappeared, all except for the gatehouse.

Brinkburn Chase   Brinkburn Priory near Rothbury and Alnwick, Northumberland was an Augustinian priory, founded in 1135. It stood, surrounded by trees, in the bottom of the valley of the river Coquet. The ruined priory church was rebuilt in the 1850s. It is a rather forbidding, fortress-like building noted for its internal colonnade and large, formidable sculpted figure of Jesus by Fenwick Lawson. It is now cared for by English Heritage.

Castle Acre   The Cluniac priory at Castle Acre, a village some 12½ miles east of King's Lynn in Norfolk, was originally sited within the castle, when founded in about 1090, but was soon relocated to its present site. The ruins of walls and towers today retain examples of late Norman architecture. The 15th-century prior's lodging, which gives the appearance of a mansion house, is impressive. This building remained in use after the dissolution of the priory in 1537.

Chetwode Avenue   Chetwode Priory, near Finmere, Buckinghamshire, was founded in 1244 by Sir Ralph de Norwich for Augustinian monks. The priory manor belonged to Nutley Abbey and after the Reformation it was granted to the Risley family, who held it from 1541 to 1755. The original church of the priory became parochial in 1480 and forms part of the chancel of the present parish church. There was once, also, a hermitage dedicated to St Stephen and St Lawrence which was founded by an ancestor of the Chetwode family.

Chicksands Avenue   A 12th-century Gilbertine priory at Chicksands, about nine miles south-east of Bedford, and a late Victorian country house at Bletchley played vital roles during the Second World War. For 400 years, both monks and nuns lived at Chicksands Priory but, at the dissolution of the monasteries in 1538, the priory became a family home and remained so for another 400 years. During the 1939-45 war, it became one of the main centres for the interception of the enemy's radio messages which were then passed to the cryptanalysts handling German air force cyphers at Bletchley Park. More recently, the priory was the home of a USAF security unit in military and counter-intelligence roles.

Chirbury Close   The village of Chirbury lies 15½ miles south-west of Shrewsbury. The *National Gazetteer* of 1868 records the remains of an Augustininian abbey founded by Robert de Boulers during the reign of Henry III and notes that the church of St Michael was formerly connected with Chirbury Priory. Following a geophysical survey in 2001, a team from Porth y Waen Study Centre carried out a series of excavations in a field next to the church at Chirbury. One of the trenches formed part of an investigation into the village that surrounded the church and its later monastery. Documentary sources had previously revealed that there was a church there in 915 and evidence has been found of the use of the site during the early Middle Ages. There seems little doubt that a medieval priory existed here. Investigations are continuing.

Culross Grove   Work on the illumination of manuscripts and on book-binding were two of the occupations of monks living in the Cistercian abbey of Culross, founded in 1217 on the Firth of Forth opposite Falkirk. By the mid-16th century the number of monks had fallen to ten. When the east choir of the abbey church was taken over as a parish church, other buildings fell into dilapidation. Restoration of the abbey church took place in the early 1800s and again in 1905, when several buildings became what they are today. It is still in use, under the care of Historic Scotland, and may be visited.

Ealing Chase   Ealing Abbey, west London was founded in 1897 as a Benedictine monastery at the invitation of Cardinal Vaughan from Downside Abbey near Bath. In 1947 it became an independent priory and was raised to abbey status by Pope Pius XII in 1955. Ealing Abbey today still supports a small but thriving community of monks.

Easby Grove   Easby Abbey, on the Heritage Trail near Great Ayton, North Yorkshire, was founded in about 1155 by the Constable of Richmond Castle. It was originally intended for 13 canons of the Premonstratensian order but was augmented in the 14th century with more canons and a hospital for 22 poor men. It was dissolved in 1537 but, unlike most monastic buildings, it never became a private home and now stands as a defiant ruin, deep in the valley of the river Swale.

Flaxley Gate   A small country house in the Forest of Dean, near Cinderford, Gloucestershire today occupies the site of the Cistercian abbey of Flaxley, founded in the mid-1150s. The abbey, which would have been listed among the smaller monasteries in the early 16th century, was possibly in partial ruin at the time of the dissolution. The abbey chapel is now the church of St Mary's, from the churchyard of which the house, which is not open to the public, can be seen.

Hurley Croft   Hurley Priory in Berkshire was founded in the mid-11th century on the site of an earlier monastery which had been destroyed by the Danes. A Benedictine cell of Westminster Abbey, the priory was endowed by Geoffrey de Mandeville as a memorial to his first wife and was dedicated to St Osmund. Only the nave of the priory church survives as the parish church of St Mary. Ladye Place now stands on the site of the priory, where there are a few remnants of 13th- and 14th-century monastic buildings.

Kilwinning Drive   Kilwinning Abbey, Ayrshire, Scotland dates from the mid-12th century, although a religious community dating back to the seventh century is believed to have existed here before it. Hugh de Morville, a wealthy landowner, founded the abbey with a community of Tyrinensian Benedectine monks from Kelso. It grew rapidly and for 400 years prospered on the income from its granges, lands and the tithes from 20 parish churches. Destroyed at the Reformation, the abbey estates passed to the earls of Eglinton, who still own them and are involved in the preservation of the abbey's substantial ruins.

Lanercost Crescent   Close to Hadrian's Wall in Cumbria, Lanercost Priory was founded in 1166 by Robert de Vaux and, with a generous endowment, Augustinian canons built a grand monastery using stones rifled from the Roman wall. Being so close to the Scottish border, the priory suffered many fierce raids during its turbulent history, ransacked first in 1280 after a visit by Edward I and, later, by William Wallace, then by King David II of Scotland in 1346. After the dissolution of the monasteries it was converted into a private house, but after 1716 all except the magnificent church fell to ruin. Today only the foundations of the east range of claustral buildings can be seen, but the west range and the prior's house still stand as does the ruined arch of the gatehouse and the partly ruined, partly restored church.

Launde   Launde Abbey, 14 miles east of Leicester, is now a retreat house and conference centre for religious, cultural and educational purposes. An Elizabethan manor house in park and woodland stands on the site of the Augustinian priory which was founded in 1119. In the upper Chater Valley, Launde Park Wood and Launde Big Wood are havens for wildlife, with many varieties of woodland and parkland birds, and are regarded as among the last reliable sites for redstarts in Leicestershire.

Leominster Gate   Nunnery … monastery … church. That, in a nutshell, is the history of religious houses at Leominster, which is 12½ miles north of Hereford. Nuns occupied the site between the ninth century and the year 1046. About a hundred years later, Leominster Priory was founded as part of the Benedictine order. In the 16th century, following the dissolution, only the nave remained, serving as a church to local parishioners which consisted of three parallel naves featuring a combination of architectural forms.

Lilleshall Avenue   The monastery known as Lilleshall Abbey was founded in the mid-12th century, five years after Arrouasian canons had moved a short distance from the place near Telford in Shropshire where they had originally settled. The new abbey, built in stone and in Romanesque style, was later complemented by Norman additions. Much of considerable architectural interest remains today.

Lindisfarne Drive   Lindisfarne, known as Holy Island, has a unique natural history and is on the Heritage Trail. A sandy wilderness off the coast of Northumberland, the island was originally designated as a nature reserve for flora, but it also attracts hundreds of birds in spring and autumn during their migration to and from the Arctic. Bird watching and wildfowling are strictly controlled. A simple monastery was founded on the island in 635 by St Aidan. A hermit, St Cuthbert, became the first bishop of the monastery, and shortly after his death the Lindisfarne Gospels were produced by Bishop Eadfrith. They are now in the British Museum, while St Cuthbert's coffin and Celtic Cross are in Durham Cathedral. The monastery was destroyed by the Vikings and the monks fled to Durham where they eventually settled. In the 11th century the Normans built a Benedictine priory here, the ruins of which can still be seen, along with those of a small 16th-century castle.

Lindores Croft   Lindores Abbey at Newburgh, north Fife, Scotland was once a wealthy abbey and more famous than Balmerino, but now it is a deserted ruin. It was founded in 1178 by a brother of William I, David, Earl of Huntingdon. The first abbot was Guido, who arrived at Lindores with 24 Benedictine monks of the Order of Tiron from Kelso Abbey, where he had been Prior. Destroyed during the Reformation, the abbey's red sandstone has been plundered over the years by house builders in Newburgh. The ruin of the north wall of the refectory remains, and in the well-kept grounds are two tiny stone coffins which contained the bodies of Robert and Henry, the infant sons of Earl David.

Little Dunmow   A priory of canons of the Augustinian order was founded in 1104 at Little Dunmow, a village just off the A120 between Bishop's Stortford and Braintree. The monastic buildings on rising ground south-

west of the church were later destroyed and only the east end of the choir of
the priory church (St Mary's) remains and forms the parish church, noted
for its Gothic windows.

Malton Close   Malton Priory stands on the north bank of the river Derwent
in North Yorkshire. The once glorious minster is now a fragment
incorporated in the Priory Church of Old Malton. The original priory was
founded in 1150 by Eustace Fitz-John for the Gilbertines, a new English
order established in 1148 by St Gilbert, a priest from Sempringham in
Lincolnshire. Both monks and nuns were included under one Superior, but
the monks professed the rule of St Augustine while the nuns professed that
of St Benedict.

Margam Crescent   Margam today is a country park with a religious history
near Port Talbot in Wales. A Cistercian abbey was founded here in the
mid-12th century by monks under the orders of St Bernard of Clairvaux.
The monastery was dissolved at the Reformation, but the abbey church has
served as the parish church since 1542. There are extensive remains in the
850-acre park, including the particularly fine Chapter House ruins.

Netley Court   The story goes that it is due to falling masonry crushing to
death an entrepeneur planning to demolish a Tudor mansion and sell the
stone, that the extensive ruins of what had begun as a Cistercian abbey
in the 13th century remain part of our heritage. The locals of Netley,
close to the left bank of Southampton Water, refused to allow the planned
destruction to proceed. It was after the dissolution that the abbey had been
converted to a mansion, which it remained for about 300 years. Much of
what remains at Netley has been described as a strange combination of
monastic architecture and elaborate, residential Tudor styling.

Parkminster   St Hughes Charterhouse is a Carthusian monastery at
Parkminster, near Horsham, Sussex. Built in the early 1870s, it was the
first Carthusian monastery to be built in England since the Reformation
and has been home to a community of Catholic monks since 1873. Living
as hermits, they spend two-thirds of their day in silence and their aim is
the perfection of love. The buildings consist of 35 hermitages linked by a
cloister, and community buildings with the church at the centre.

Penmon Close   Holy Penmon, an isolated spot on the east coast of Anglesey,
was where St Seirid formed a monastery. It was further developed over the
centuries until, by the 10th, it included a wooden church building. This was
destroyed by Viking raids in the late 900s. It was rebuilt in stone during
the 12th century and today remains the most complete building of its age
in north-west Wales. Cruciform-shaped, the oldest part, the nave, was
completed in 1140 and other additions followed over the next 100 years.
The monastery was dissolved in 1537 but the church remained. Further
rebuilding took place in the 19th century.

Pershore Croft   Pershore Abbey in Worcestershire stands on the site of a seventh-century monastery which was ravaged by the Danes in AD 958 and a Benedictine abbey which was destroyed by fire in 1002. A new abbey church was built in about 1100 and this, with much repair and restoration work over the centuries, is incorporated in the building which stands today on the edge of the town. Skilful restoration by Sir Gilbert Scott in the 19th century and Sir Harold Brakspear in 1914 managed to save and enhance much of the craftsmanship and many of the medieval features of the Norman abbey.

St Bartholomews   Now known as the Royal Hospital of St Bartholomew, or Bart's, this was founded in 1123 by Rahere, one of Henry I's courtiers who, after he was taken ill on a pilgrimage to Rome, was inspired by a vision of St Bartholomew and vowed to found a hospital for the poor in London. He also built a church and Augustinian priory at Smithfield.

St Bees   At the village of St Bees, Cumbria, the ancient church dedicated to St Mary and St Bega is all that remains of a Benedictine priory founded in about 1120, during the reign of Henry I. A cell of St Mary's Abbey, York, it was built on the site of an earlier monastic building dating back to about the 10th century which was probably destroyed by the Vikings. Following the Reformation, the roof of the fine Norman priory church was pillaged and the building fell prey to the weather.

St Botolph's   Founded at the end of the 11th century in conjunction with an existing Anglo-Saxon minster, St Botolph's Priory in Colchester, Essex was the first Augustinian priory to be built in England. Believed to have been a placid, uneventful community of no great wealth or eminence, St Botolph's was dissolved in 1536. The claustral buildings changed hands several times over the years before they decayed and eventually disappeared, except for a few fragmented remains. The priory church became the parish church and burial ground. Much of the west front and a large part of the nave are still standing.

Shrewsbury Close   The Benedictine Abbey of St Peter and St Paul, Shrewsbury, Shropshire was founded in 1083 by Roger de Montgomery and built on the site of a wooden Saxon church. In 1283 a Parliament met in the Chapter House, the first national assembly in which the Commons had any share by legal authority. The Benedictine monks followed their routine of study, prayer and manual work centred round the church for 457 years. After dissolution in 1540, only the nave remained to serve as the parish church. Today, Shrewsbury Abbey is renowned as the home of the fictional *Brother Cadfael*.

Stanbrook Place   Stanbrook Abbey, Worcester is today a community of Benedictine nuns dedicated to the praise and service of God and the Church and reverence for creation, which they express through literary work, art, music, book-binding and printing. In 2003 there were 28 professed nuns and two postulates. The community was founded in Flanders in 1623 and has been resident at Stanbrook since 1838.

Stavordale   Stavordale Priory near Charlton Musgrove in Somerset was founded in the 13th century. It fell into disuse but was rescued from decay in the early 20th century and restored as a private house.

Tewkesbury Lane   The vast Norman abbey at Tewkesbury, Gloucestershire was, in its heyday, one of the richest monasteries in England. It was established on the site where in the eighth century there had been a small Saxon monastery by monks of the Benedictine order some 300 years later. When the abbey was surrendered at the dissolution most of its buildings were demolished, but townspeople bought the church to use as their parish church – the second largest in England. Several restorations have taken place and today it provides a wealth of architectural interest to the visitor.

Tynemouth Place   On the headland overlooking the river Tyne, Tynemouth Priory Church of the Blessed Virgin and St Oswin stands together with the castle, the remains of a Second World War gun battery and the regional coastguards' observational centre. Originally built as a wooden chapel in AD 627, the priory church was rebuilt in stone in 633, since when it has been reconstructed many times after periods of abandonment. The remains of three kings are buried here – Oswin AD 651, Osric 792 and Malcolm of Scotland 1093. The priory is now cared for by English Heritage.

Ulverscroft   Deep in the ancient Charnwood Forest near Markfield, Leicestershire are the ruins of Ulverscroft Priory. It was founded in about 1130 by Robert Bossu, a Norman Earl of Leicester, for monks of the Augustinian order. Henry VIII at first gave Ulverscroft a short reprieve during the Reformation, but it was eventually dissolved in 1539. There is also a nature reserve at Ulverscroft which is managed by the Leicestershire and Rutland Trust for Nature Conservation. Access is by permit only.

Wadhurst Lane   Linking Monkston to Kents Hill, this road is named after the village of Wadhurst, East Sussex. However, it can also be linked to the monastery theme. A modern priory, St Benedictine's was founded at Royston, Hertfordshire in 1916. It was moved to Wadhurst, Sussex in 1964 where it remained until 1994, when it moved to Cobh in County Cork, Ireland because the Bishop of Cloyne wanted a Benedictine monastic presence to provide a retreat and bible garden in his diocese.

Waltham Drive   Waltham Abbey church today is the remnant of an ecclesiastical settlement here which goes back to the days of King Canute. In the early 11th century, Harold Godwinson (later King Harold II) founded a college for secular canons and a new church in which to house a 'miraculous' stone cross found in Somerset by Canute's standard bearer, Tovi the Proud. Harold believed that it was the powers of this cross that cured him of the paralysis from which he suffered. After his death in 1066 at Hastings, Harold was buried behind the high altar at Waltham. Over the years the status of the abbey increased. Ironically, this is where Henry VIII first met Thomas Cranmer – the dissolution of the monasteries and the Reformation of the church followed a short time later. Waltham Abbey was the last to fall, in 1540.

Waverley Croft Waverley Abbey, south-west of Guildford between Farnham and Godalming, was the first Cistercian abbey to be established in England. In 1128, William Giffard, Bishop of Winchester, granted 60 acres of land for its foundation, and Abbot John and 12 Cistercian monks from France were its first inhabitants. The abbey church took 150 years to build and achieved considerable wealth and power. The monastery survived the Black Death, a period of famine in the 14th century and repeated flooding from the river Wey over 400 years, until it was dissolved in 1536. It was then acquired by the Earl of Southampton who dismantled it and used some of the stone to build Loseley House nearby. The rest has been gradually taken for use in other buildings and all that remains are a few monastic arches. It is said that Sir Walter Scott took his inspiration for his *Waverley* novels from Waverley Abbey.

Welbeck Close Welbeck Abbey, near Worksop, Nottinghamshire, is now a landscaped park with a stately mansion, once seat of the dukes of Portland. There is a garden centre in the grounds and a Defence Academy in the house. This is a residential sixth-form college established in 1953 for young men and women intent on an Army career. Scarcely anything remains of the original abbey which was founded in about 1154 by Thomas de Cuckney for Premonstratensian canons from Newhouse Abbey in Lincolnshire.

Woodspring Court Founded in the early part of the 13th century, Woodspring Priory is near the north Somerset resort of Weston-super-Mare, by the mouth of the river Severn. It was owned by a division of the Order of St Augustine and it is thought that monks from the priory founded the church at nearby Locking in the latter part of the 13th century. Ruins of the priory today form part of a farmhouse.

Wymondham Wymondham Abbey in Norfolk was founded in 1107 by William d'Albini, Chief Butler to Henry I, as a priory of the great Benedictine monastery of St Albans. A great church and claustral accommodation for the monks was built with stone imported from Caen. It became an abbey in 1488 but was suppressed and the monastic buildings destroyed by Henry VIII in 1538, since when the surviving parts of the abbey church with its 20th-century restoration has served as Wymondham parish church. Wymondham Abbey is on the Heritage Trail.

NEWLANDS

Newlands Farm and its land, from which this name is taken, stood adjacent to Willen Road in Little Woolstone. Now an area of parkland opposite Willen Lake, it contains a tree cathedral, tennis centre, pitch-and-putt and the Gulliver's Land theme park.

THEME **Voyagers**

Frobisher Gate   Sir Martin Frobisher (*c*.1535-94) was sent to sea as a boy and grew up with the dream of finding a north-west passage to Cathay. On 7 June 1576 he set sail northwards with 35 men on two ships. After almost being lost off the coast of Greenland, they reached Labrador on 28 July. In 1585 Frobisher was with Drake's expedition to the West Indies and was knighted for his services against the Spanish Armada. Sailing near Brest in 1594, he was wounded and died at Plymouth on 22 November.

Livingstone Drive   David Livingstone (1813-73) was a Scottish missionary and traveller. He worked in a cotton mill from the age of 10 until he was 24, when his yearning for missionary work inspired him to study medicine in London. His missionary travels in Africa led to many discoveries including the Victoria Falls of Zambezi.

The central 'aisle' of the Cathedral of Trees at Newlands.

NORTHFIELD

Named after 'The Great North Field' which covered an extensive area of the medieval parish of Milton Keynes and is shown on a 1685 map.

Northfield Drive is the only named road on this industrial estate from which a number of companies operate, including Coca-Cola, Evans, Halshaw, Honda and Jaguar.

OLD FARM PARK

Old Farm Park takes the name of a farm, The Old Farm, which was at Walton End, Wavendon until, with no consideration for its historic connections, it was heartlessly razed to the ground in April 2005.

THEME **Holst Crescent runs through from Browns Wood to Old Farm Park and continues the theme of Composers of Classical Music. Musicians Sir John Dankworth and Dame Cleo Laine live at the Old Rectory, Wavendon, where they founded the now famous Wavendon All Music Plan at The Stables in 1970. They have greatly enhanced the musical life of Milton Keynes.**

Sir John Dankworth CBE and Dame Cleo Laine.

Arne Lane   Thomas Arne (1710-78) was an English composer born in London and educated at Eton. His father was an upholsterer who wished his son to be a lawyer, but Thomas developed as an accomplished violinist. His sister was the actress, Mrs Cibber, and he gave her a part in his first opera, *Rosamond.* Arne was engaged as composer to Drury Lane Theatre, where he wrote famous settings of Shakespearean songs such as *Under the Greenwood Tree, Where the Bee Sucks* and *Blow, Blow Thou Winter Wind,* but his most famous song is *Rule Britannia.*

Balfe Mews   Michael William Balfe (1808-70) was an English composer born in Dublin. He began composing at the age of six and made his debut as a violinist when he was eight. He came to London in 1823 and wrote the music for a ballet, *La Perouse,* which was performed in Milan. He sang in the Italian Opera in Paris. His voice was a pure, rich baritone. On his return to England, Balfe was appointed conductor of the London Italian Opera. He wrote many operas, operettas and other music. He died at Rowley Abbey, his estate in Hertfordshire.

Beethoven Close   Ludwig von Beethoven (1770-1827) was a German composer born in Bonn. He had a miserable childhood at the hands of a father who wanted to turn him into a profitable child prodigy, like Mozart. As a man, he was eccentric, unkempt and arrogant, which made him unpopular with Viennese society. He studied under Mozart and Haydn and his early works are similar in style, but his later works are products of the Romantic Movement prevailing at the time and reflect the climate of the Napoleonic Wars. He suffered from progressive deafness from 1798 onwards.

Bellini Close   Vincenzo Bellini (1801-35), Italian operatic composer, was born in Catania, Sicily, the son of an organist. He studied at the Conservatorio of Naples under the patronage of a Sicilian nobleman. He wrote fluent, expressive melodies which were much admired by his friend, Chopin, and was always sympathetic to the natural charm of the human voice and its technical abilities. Bellini was idolised in Italy, but died aged only 34 in Paris.

Borodin Court   Alexander Borodin (1833-87) was a Russian composer and scientist. He was the illegitimate son of a prince, who registered him as the child of a serf. He was composing by the age of nine, but was trained for medicine and became a distinguished chemist. He studied music seriously in 1862, after which he wrote three symphonies and operas, including the unfinished *Prince Igor* from which come the well-known 'Polovtsian Dances'. Borodin died from a burst artery in his heart.

Boyce Crescent   William Boyce (1710-79) was an English composer born in London. In 1736 he was appointed composer to the Chapel Royal, and organist in 1758. He is highly rated as a composer of church music. His works include the song *Hearts of Oak* and he compiled and edited a *Collection of Cathedral Music*. Boyce was the son of a cabinet maker and a choirboy at St Paul's Cathedral and became partially deaf at a young age. He also became Master of the King's Musick and wrote two musical entertainments which were performed at Drury Lane. He is buried beneath the dome of St Paul's.

Brahms Close   Johannes Brahms (1833-97) was a German composer. The son of a poor orchestral musician, he was a talented pianist and to earn a living played in Hamburg's dockside inns. He began composing piano sonatas, which Schumann encouraged him to publish. He was so grateful that after Schumann died Brahms took care of his widow and children for as long as necessary. He led a quiet life, giving occasional concerts of his music, which ranged from symphonies, concertos and choral works to quintets, quartets and trios, plus a lot of piano music and songs.

Britten Grove   Benjamin Britten (1913-76) was born Baron Benjamin Britten of Aldeburgh. An English composer, he studied under John Ireland during the 1930s and wrote much incidental music for documentary films and plays. He also composed large-scale instrumental works, vocal and choral music. Among his best-known works are his *Young Person's Guide to the Orchestra*, and his operas *Peter Grimes*, *Billy Budd* and *Gloriana*, which he composed for the Coronation of Queen Elizabeth II. His children's operas include *The Little Sweep* and *Let's Make an Opera*. In 1948 Britten co-founded the annual Aldeburgh Festival. He was made a Companion of Honour in 1953, awarded the Order of Merit in 1965 and given a life peerage in 1976.

Bruckner Gardens   Anton Bruckner (1824-96) was an Austrian composer. He started as a choirboy at the Monastery of Saint Florian where he learned the organ and became assistant organist and then organist. He studied in Vienna and was appointed organist at Linz Cathedral. He composed nine symphonies, four masses, a large number of smaller sacred pieces and many choral works.

Byrd Crescent   William Byrd (1543-1623) was an English composer born in Lincolnshire. Little is known of his early life, but at the age of 20 he was organist of Lincoln Cathedral for nine years until 1572. He was then joint organist with Tallis of the Chapel Royal. Despite being a Catholic, he managed to stay in favour with Queen Elizabeth I and got away with composing Catholic masses and motets as well as Anglican services, psalm settings and anthems, pieces for the virginals and solo songs. Byrd is known as the father of keyboard music.

Curzon Place   Sir Clifford Curzon (1907-82) was a British pianist. He studied with Schnabel in Berlin and made his debut at the Queen's Hall, London when he was 16. Curzon was particularly well-known for his interpretations of Beethoven, Mozart and Schubert. He was knighted in 1977.

Davenport Lea   Possibly refers to Francis William Davenport, composer of piano and violin music, who died in 1925 aged 77. Alternatively, Pembroke Davenport was a composer, musical director, arranger and conductor of Broadway musicals such as *Show Boat* (1946), *Kiss Me Kate* (1948-51) and *Pal Joey* (1965).

Farjeon Court   Harry Farjeon (1878-1948) was an English composer, musician and teacher, with a prolific output of popular light music. He was very popular in the early 20th century but has now been largely forgotten and his music is rarely performed, although his piano pieces might be found in second-hand shops. In his day, his music was admired and premiered at the Proms. He was the brother of Eleanor Farjeon the writer.

Goldmark Close   Carl Goldmark (1830-1915) was a Hungarian composer who studied in Vienna and wrote lavish operas such as *Merlin* and *The Queen of Sheba*, for which he is mainly remembered. He also wrote two symphonies, two violin concertos and other music. His nephew, Rubin Goldmark (1872-1936), was an American composer who taught Gershwin and Copland.

Greatheed Dell   The Rev. Samuel Stephenson Greatheed was an organist and arranger of church music. His father, the Rev. Samuel Greatheed, also an organist, was a vicar at Sherington in the 18th century, having been trained for the ministry at the Academy of the Rev. William Bull in nearby Newport Pagnell. He married Jane Stephenson, daughter of the Rev. Christopher Stephenson, vicar of Olney, and was a close associate of William Cowper.

Handel Mead   George Frederick Handel (1685-1759) was a German-born English composer. At the age of 17 he was organist of Halle Cathedral and also a violinist and keyboard player. He became a naturalised Englishman after settling here in 1712 and is regarded as our greatest composer. He worked as Director of the newly founded Royal Academy of Music and of Covent Garden Opera House. Handel's *Messiah, Water Music* and *Music for the Royal Fireworks* were all written especially for King George I. He composed numerous concertos, suites and oratorios and his music helped to fund the building of the Foundling Hospital with Thomas Coram and William Hogarth. He performed charity concerts in the Foundling Hospital chapel, where he was organist, and taught music to the children, some of whom appeared in his works and succeeded him as chapel organists.

Hindemith Gardens   Paul Hindemith (1895-1963) was a German composer who first found fame as a viola player. At the age of 11 he ran away from home because his parents were against his musical ambitions. He played a variety of instruments in cafés and dance halls, but the viola was his main instrument. He then worked as a teacher in Berlin. His compositions during the 1920s were regarded as extremist modernism and his music was banned by the Nazi regime in 1933. He went to America in 1939. His works include operas, a ballet, many concertos, sonatas and much utility music.

Irving Dale   Irving Berlin (real name Israel Baline) was an American composer born in Russia in 1888 and taken by his parents to America when he was a baby. He worked as a singing waiter before finding fame with his songs, such as *Alexander's Ragtime Band*. His first, lesser known musicals were written for the stage, but his great success came in films such as *Annie Get Your Gun* and *White Christmas*.

Kalman Gardens   Emmerich Kalman (1882-1953) was a Hungarian composer of operettas, which included *The Gay Hussars*. His career was overshadowed by the greater popularity of Franz Lehar.

Ketelbey Nook   Albert Ketelbey (1875-1959) was an English composer born in Birmingham. By the time he was a teenager, he was composing classical pieces. He went to Trinity College of Music, where he beat Holst in a scholarship competition. He composed choral and chamber music and descriptive pieces, which were in the popular impressionistic style of the late 19th and early 20th centuries. Ketelbey's works include *In a Persian Market* and *In a Chinese Temple Garden*.

Lutyens Grove   (Agnes) Elisabeth Lutyens (1906-86) was a British composer of orchestral and chamber music. Her early compositions were not well received. In the 1950s, she wrote a chamber opera, *Infidelio*, and a cantata, *De Amore*, but neither was performed until 1973. In later years she was accepted as a leading British composer. She was made a Companion of the British Empire in 1969 and is the daughter of the architect, Sir Edwin Lutyens.

Morley Crescent   Thomas Morley (1557-1603) was organist at St Paul's Cathedral and, like so many of the great musicians of his time, was a Gentleman of the Chapel Royal. He also composed songs for Shakespeare's plays and wrote *A Plaine and Easi Introduction to Practicall Musicke* (1597) which was popular for 200 years and is still in print as the best source of information on 16th-century music. Morley wrote church music, instrumental music, lute songs and many fine madrigals.

Nielson Court   Carl August Nielsen (1865-1931) was a Danish composer born near Odense. He was the son of a house painter who was also a village fiddler. He studied at Copenhagen Conservatoire before writing six symphonies, a tragic opera, a comic opera, chamber music, concertos for flute, clarinet and violin and a huge organ work, *Commotio*, which was his last work before he died in 1931. Nielsen was Denmark's greatest 20th-century composer. He was also a conductor and had a big influence on the musical development of Denmark.

Novello Croft   Ivor Novello Davies (1893-1951) was a Welsh composer, song-writer, actor and dramatist. He wrote many well-known songs, musicals and plays and was very popular on the London stage during the 1920s to 1940s. His plays include *The Dancing Years* and *Kings Rhapsody* and one of his most enduring songs is *Keep the Home Fires Burning*.

Protheroe Field   Daniel Protheroe (1866-1934) was a Welsh/American composer of religious music. Although he emigrated to America in 1885, he is still much honoured by the Welsh town of Ystradgynlais, where a roadside marker commemorates his birthplace.

Quilter Meadow   Roger Quilter (1877-1953) was an English composer born in Brighton. After studying in Germany, he devoted all his life to composition, making no public appearances and holding no official posts. He is best known for his songs, but also composed an opera, *Julia*, a radio opera, *The Blue Boar*, and *The Children's Overture* which is based on nursery rhymes.

Rackstraw Grove   This possibly refers to William Smyth Rockstro (1823-95), who was originally named Rackstraw. A friend of Mendelssohn, he was a musical theorist and archaeologist, an authority on plainsong and author of several books, including a life of Handel. Another possibility is the fictitious character, Ralph Rackstraw, from Gilbert and Sullivan's operetta, *HMS Pinafore*.

Ravel Close   Maurice Ravel (1875-1937) was a French composer of Swiss descent, best known nowadays for his *Bolero*. In his early days he was regarded as a rebel and his compositions met with disapproval. By the beginning of the 20th century, his piano music had become very popular and he went on to write the music for the Diaghilev ballet *Daphnis et Chloe*. Operas, orchestral music and piano suites followed. In 1933 Ravel was found to have a brain tumour and he composed no more. He was born in the Basque region of France, hence the Spanish flavour to much of his music.

Rodwell Gardens   George Herbert Rodwell (1800-52) was a prolific composer for the theatre. He was proprietor of the Adelphi theatre, London and, later, Director of Music at Covent Garden. His works include musical adaptations for the stage of literary works such as Sir Walter Scott's *The Lord of the Isles* and Charles Dickens's *A Christmas Carol*. Dickens is said to have been present at the rehearsals.

Rossini Place   Gioacchino Antonio Rossini (1792-1868) was the Italian composer of 36 highly successful operas including *The Barber of Seville*, *William Tell* and *The Thieving Magpie*. He gave up serious composing after the age of 37, but wrote a number of smaller works which are collectively called *Sins of My Old Age*. He enjoyed food and invented a number of recipes, such as Tournedos Rossini.

Tansman Lane   Alexander Tansman (1897-1986) was a Polish composer. A concert of his music in Paris in 1920 first brought him to the public's attention. He settled in Paris but travelled widely, conducting and giving piano performances of his own compositions. He wrote seven symphonies, several piano concertos, string quartets, songs, operas and ballets. There are both French and Polish characteristics in his style. He spent the Second World War in America and then returned to Paris.

Taverner Close   John Taverner (1495-1545) was an English musician, organist at Boston and at Christ Church, Oxford who composed masses and motets. He was accused of heresy and imprisoned by Cardinal Wolsey but was released because he was 'but a musician'. After about four years at Oxford, he gave up music and settled in Boston, Lincolnshire, where he was one of Thomas Cromwell's chief agents in the suppression of the monasteries and the martyrdom of religious opponents. He died in Boston aged about 50 years. Much of Taverner's fine church music is still published and played today.

Verdi Close   Giuseppe Verdi (1813-1901), Italian composer of operas, was the son of a village innkeeper, and started composing in childhood. The performance of his first opera, *Oberto*, at La Scala, Milan set him on the road to success. *La Traviata* and *Rigoletto* followed and then *Aida* was commissioned for the new Cairo opera house, which was built to celebrate the opening of the Suez Canal. Verdi wrote his last opera, *Falstaff,* when he was 79 years old. Also an organist, he was a country-loving man who led a simple life, despite his great wealth, and he founded a home for aged musicians in Milan.

Webber Heath   In view of the fact that Milton Keynes Development Corporation decreed that no road should be named after a living person, this cannot be Andrew Lloyd-Webber. The intended must have been Carl Maria Friedrich Ernst von Weber, a German composer and pianist, who was born of an impoverished noble Austrian family in 1786. He learned the piano as a child and his second opera was performed when he was 13. He directed various opera companies and orchestras and composed many operettas, operas, songs, symphonies and concertos and two masses. His last and most acclaimed work, *Oberon,* was commissioned for Covent Garden theatre and was performed there in 1826. A few months later, Weber died in London from exhaustion.

Wishart Green   Peter Wishart (1921-84) was a British composer, conductor and accompanist. He also had an academic career as a lecturer at Birmingham School of Music and the Guildhall School of Music before becoming a Professor at Reading University. Wishart wrote an opera, *The Clandestine Marriage*, many songs, religious and other vocal music as well as orchestral works. He composed a festal *Te Deum* to commemorate the coronation of Queen Elizabeth II and a choral symphony, *Then Out of the Sweet Warm Weather.*

PENNYLAND

Named after the existing 'Pennyland Field' shown on a 1678 map of Great Linford and on Ordnance Survey maps 205 and 236. Historically, pennyland was land valued at a penny a year.

THEME Old Coins

Angel Close   The Angel was a gold coin which came into being in the reign of Edward IV. In 1465, the value of the existing Noble (six shillings and eight pence) was raised to ten shillings, so the Angel was introduced as the lower denomination coin. The angel St Michael slaying a dragon was on the obverse, with a ship on the reverse. It ceased to exist after the reign of Charles I.

Boodle Close   Boodle is counterfeit money, or money obtained by corruption, or money or valuables which have been stolen or used as a bribe.

Broad Piece   The Broadpiece (or Broad) was a gold 20-shilling coin introduced during the Commonwealth (1649-60) by Cromwell. It bore the head of Oliver on the obverse, with a crowned shield on the reverse. It was dated 1656 and engraved by Thomas Simon.

Carolus Close   A Carolus was any coin of the reign of Charles I which bore his portrait on the obverse and, on the reverse, a lion rampant, a harp, three leopards and a fleur-de-lys within the four quarters of an oval shield.

Florin Close   The Florin was originally a Florentine gold coin struck in the 13th century, with a lily on the obverse. It was first struck in Britain in 1344, but discarded until it was reintroduced, 500 years later, by Queen Victoria. An English silver, or cupro-nickel, florin worth a tenth of a pound, was minted in 1849 and for many years after. It became known as the two-shilling piece, which was replaced by the ten-pence piece with decimalisation in 1971. The Florin ceased as legal tender when the ten-pence piece was reduced in size.

Leopard Drive   The Leopard, or half florin, was created in 1344 on the instructions of Edward III. It was a gold coin with a value of three shillings, but was rejected by the people because the gold used to strike it had been over-valued. It was recalled later the same year and melted down. As most of them were destroyed, it is a very rare coin. A leopard on the obverse gave the coin its name.

Longcross   Long Cross coinage was the penny coinage introduced in 1247 by Henry III in place of short cross coinage. On the reverse of the pennies was a cross, which had to be lengthened to bring it to the edge of the coins to prevent them being clipped by crooks, who removed some of the metal and then passed on the coin at its original value.

Noble Close   The Noble was a gold coin which replaced the unsuccesful Leopard in Edward III's reign. Its value was six shillings and eight pence. On the obverse it depicted the king aboard a ship and on the reverse a cruciform design. Also in gold, smaller denominations were the half-noble and the quarter-noble. Changing in value and design, the Noble was in circulation for about 150 years.

Quadrans Close   A Quadrans (plural Quadrantes) was a Roman copper coin, worth the fourth part of an As, which was a copper coin of higher value.

Shilling Close   The silver Shilling, originally called the testoon, was first introduced by Henry VII in 1504, but did not become real currency until the reign of Edward VI. By the early 17th century it had been established as an important denomination and was produced in large quantities thereafter. Its real silver content was greatly reduced over the centuries and it was replaced by the five pence piece with decimalisation in 1971.

Skeats Wharf   This is a close and footpath leading down to the Grand Union canal with its wharf. Sceats were silver coins introduced in the late seventh century. They were small and thick, about half an inch in diameter and weighed up to 20 grains. Sceats were replaced by the silver penny at the end of the eighth century.

The Grand Union canal runs through Milton Keynes and provides a tranquil setting for housing at Pennyland, in the north-east of the city.

Sovereign Drive. The Sovereign is a gold coin first introduced by Henry VII in 1489. Its value was 20 shillings and it was based on a Dutch coin called the *real d'or* and originally known as the double-ryal. The quality of the striking of the Sovereign has generally been very high and it has become an important coin in the trading of gold bullion throughout the world.

Staters Pound   Staters were ancient Greek standard coins of various sorts. They included the gold daric and the silver tetradrachm. The word 'stater' originally meant a pound weight.

Sterling Close   Sterling denotes the fineness of silver; it is the British standard of 925 parts silver per 1,000 parts total. British Sterling Silver coins were struck until 1919, after which the metal content was changed to 500 parts fine silver. Sterling also now means British money of standard value.

PINEHAM

Named after Pineham Farm, which lay to the east of Milton Keynes village and is shown on Ordnance Survey map 171. This is the site of Cotton Valley sewage works, which is surrounded by parkland where there is a helipad and BMX track.

TONGWELL

Tongwell was an old field name, Tongwell Close, shown on an 1806 map of Newport Pagnell, Ordnance Survey 27. There are also Tongwell Farm, Tongwell Brook, which flows into the river Ouzel at Newport Pagnell, and Tongwell Lake, which has water-skiing facilities.

THEME **American States**

Delaware Drive   Although one of the smallest states, Delaware is one of the most heavily industrialised. Wilmington, the administrative centre of several large chemical companies, is known as the chemical capital of the world. Also manufactured in Delaware are motors, synthetic rubber, textiles and food products.

Maryland Road   A state on the eastern seaboard of America, manufacturing is most important to Maryland's economy. Metals, metal products and food processing are among its industries.

Michigan Drive   A state in the north central region of the USA, Michigan is bordered by the Great Lakes. Most of its commerce is in the Lower Peninsula area where Detroit is well known for its motor industry. Iron and steel, machinery and chemicals are also produced.

Vermont Place   In the north-east of the USA in New England, Vermont's forests and green mountains are a popular tourist area. Its industries range from farming and market gardening to the mining of stone, sand and gravel and the manufacturing of wood and paper.

WALNUT TREE

The name is taken from Walnut Tree Farm, a listed 16th-century, part timber-framed farmhouse with 18th-century additions. The house still stands and is the home of the Hooton family, who have been farmers in the area for many years. Before it was surrounded by Milton Keynes, the house enjoyed the prospect of open countryside which once was famous for its walnut trees and the crops they produced. The farm barns are now used by a garden centre and animal feeds shop.

THEME **(1) Wild Flowers and Herbs**
(2) Turnpike Trusts. By the 18th century the highways had become such terrible quagmires, especially in wet weather, that local companies, or Turnpike Trusts, were set up to improve and maintain

the roads. A toll was charged for use of the roads and toll-gates set up as collection points.

Angelica Court   Wild Angelica is a tall perennial with purplish stems and pom-poms of white or pink flowers from July to September. It grows in damp, grassy places, in woods and on cliffs. The Garden Angelica usually has green stems with aromatic stalks which are crystalised and used for decorating cakes and sweet desserts. The flowers are greenish-yellow and the plant grows particularly well by the sea.

Balsam Close   Balsams are a family of flowers. They are annuals with fleshy stems, oval leaves and flowers in long, stalked spikes. The colours of the flowers are varied. There is the pink Himalayan balsam, the yellow touch-me-not balsam, the cream-coloured small balsam and the orange balsam.

Beech Fern   The Beech Fern, which grows in the rich, moist woodlands of North America, is very similar to our common bracken. It has fronds 6-10 inches long arranged in the shape of an arrow head. It has spores on the underside of the leaflets, grows persistently and at random and is deciduous.

Berberis Close   The common Berberis (vulgaris) is a spiny shrub which grows in hedges and copses. It has strings of yellow flowers from April to June and oblong red berries which are rather acidic and used in jam making. Flies, bees, beetles and some butterflies enjoy the nectar and often get covered in pollen in the process.

Bergamot Gardens   Bergamot is a small Asian tree with sour, pear-shaped fruit. The fruit rind is used to make essence of Bergamot, which is an oil used in perfumery. Another variety of Bergamot is a Mediterranean mint which yields a similar oil.

Birdlip Lane   Birdlip in Gloucestershire is a village on the old Gloucester to Cirencester road. An Act for improving and repairing the road from Gloucester to the top of Birdlip Hill and from the foot of Birdlip Hill to Crickley Hill was passed in 1806.

Blackberry   The blackberry is the fruit of the common bramble, which grows in hedgerows, fields and on heaths. It has white flowers in early summer and the black berries produced in early autumn are used to make jam, or mixed with apple for fruit pies.

Bluebell Croft   Bluebells are woodland bulbs grown in shady places beneath trees. Their blue, bell-shaped flowers from April to May are very fragrant over a short period.

Bourton Low   Bourton today is a village just outside Swindon, Wiltshire on the Oxford to Swindon road (now the A420). The turnpike trust responsible for the length of old road between Chapel-on-the-Heath and Bourton was set up by an Act dated 1723 which was renewed in 1734.

Boxberry Gardens   The box is a small evergreen tree or shrub, which grows to about 15 feet. It has spiny, leathery, oval-shaped leaves and clusters of greenish-yellow flowers from March to May. Its fruit, or berry, is small and dry.

Calamus Court   Calamus is the Latin name of a genus of palms. Their stems are used to make canes, or rattans. In ancient times the stems were made into reed pens for writing. Calamus is also the traditional name for the sweet-flag.

Camomile Court   Camomile grows to about six inches and has finely divided leaves and cream, daisy-like flowers which give off a fruity scent. In the Middle Ages, the flowers were used in monastic infirmaries to make a sedative tea and to soothe persistent headaches. A member of the daisy family, the camomile has several varieties. The stinking camomile has a sickly smell; the corn camomile grows in clumps in cornfields and is visible after harvest; the lawn camomile, a spreading perennial with a pleasant aroma, grows in grassy and heathy places.

Candlewicks   Candlewick is a material woven from tufted cotton and mainly used for making bedspreads.

Caraway Close   Caraway is a biennial aromatic herb with white flowers in June and July. It is found growing in grassy places and its seeds are used to flavour cakes.

Celandine Court   The lesser celandine is a kind of buttercup. A small, wild plant with burnished gold, star-like flowers which may be seen as early as February on sunny banks, under hedges or on roadsides. The greater celandine is not related but is a kind of poppy. It has small, yellow flowers, leaves shaped like an oak leaf and the straight stems have a yellow juice which is very acrid and poisonous. It flowers from May to August and is found in hedgerows and on wasteland near housing.

Cinnamon Grove   Cinnamon is a tropical Asian tree with aromatic yellowish-brown bark. The spice obtained from the bark is used for flavouring food, especially in Christmas cakes and puddings and in drinks, such as punch.

Cloudberry   The cloudberry is a member of the rose family. It is a low, creeping perennial with white flowers from June to August and an orange fruit. It is similar to the blackberry, but grows in upland bogs and damp moorlands.

Comfrey Close   Comfrey is of the borage family and there are eight varieties. The common comfrey is a tall, stout perennial with fairly broad leaves running down onto winged stems. The bell-shaped flowers are creamy white or mauve, growing in forked clusters in May and June. Comfrey has a black, shiny fruit and it grows by fresh water and on fenland.

Coriander Court   Coriander is a herb commonly used in cooking. The plant grows up to two feet and has pale flowers of pinkish white and bright green feathery leaves. Coriander has been used as a flavouring herb for centuries, the leaves in salads as well as in hot dishes, the seeds once used in bread-making. It is a member of the carrot family and is aromatic when ripe.

Cranberry Close   The cranberry is a low-growing, slender, creeping evergreen undershrub. It has dark green, pointed, oval leaves, pink flowers from June to August and edible, round or pear-shaped red berries, which are used to make jam or cranberry sauce.

Dunchurch Dale   Dunchurch near Daventry, Warwickshire is a picturesque village just off the A5 Watling Street on the A45/M45, three miles south of Rugby. The Old Stratford to Dunchurch Turnpike seems to have been established between 1708 and 1713. The toll-gate is said to have been near the Dunchurch school chapel.

Fyfield Barrow   Fyfield, or Fifield, meaning five hides of land, is in Oxfordshire on the Oxford to Swindon road (now the A420). The Fyfield District Turnpike Trust was set up by an Act of 1800. The St John's Bridge to Fyfield Turnpike Trust was set up by an Act of 1732 and renewed in 1738.

Goldilocks   Goldilocks is a species of buttercup, similar to a slender meadow buttercup. A short perennial, it has a few flowers with purple-tinged petals in April and May. It grows in woods and under hedges. There is a smaller variety found on mountainsides and a goldilocks aster, which is a short-medium perennial with clustered yellow flowerheads, found between September and November in woods, grassy places and on rocks by the sea.

Groundsel Close   Groundsel is very common everywhere in Britain. It has small, grey-green leaves and groups of tiny yellow flowers which are followed by fluffy pappus attached to the seeds (like dandelions). These are carried by the wind, which is why it is so prolific. A favourite food of rabbits, groundsel may be found in flower most of the year.

Harebell Close   The harebell is a wild flower of the bellflower family. It is a slender plant with blue flowers in loose clusters on long, thin stalks from July to October. It is daintier than the bluebell and is found in dry grassland and on heathland.

Hartwort Close   Hartwort is of the carrot family and is a medium-tall plant with coarse, hairy stems, small leaf clusters and white clustered flowers from June to August. A wild flower, it grows in grassy, waste places.

Highgate Over   Turnpike trusts took control of most of the main roads of London in the 18th century. Highgate stands at the beginning of the A1. The *Old Gate House Inn* in the High Street, the highest point in Highgate, is named in memory of the old toll-house which once stood there.

Hindhead Knoll   Hindhead in Surrey is on the London to Portsmouth road, now the A3. In 1749, the Sussex Turnpike Trust was established to maintain the road from Hindhead Heath to Chichester. A knoll is a round hillock, or the top of a hill.

Hockliffe Brae   Hockliffe is on the A5 (Watling Street) just north of Dunstable. Hockliffe-Two Mile Ash Turnpike was created by an Act of Parliament as early as 1706, the first local act of its kind. A 14-mile stretch of Watling Street in 1705 was almost impassable, with ruts two to three feet deep and mud everywhere. A Board of Trustees was set up to erect turnpikes, charge tolls and use

Walnut Tree Farm.

the money to repair the road. By 1824 about 200 commercial stagecoaches a week visited Hockliffe, which was at the junction of Watling Street with the Newport, Northampton, Leicester and Nottingham road (now the A4012). By 1830 there were 468 coaches a week, of which about 280 came on to Stony Stratford, as well as hundreds of private coaches, wagons and strings of pack-horses.

Huckleberry Close   The huckleberry is a shrub native to North America, where it can be seen growing on decomposing tree-stumps in woodland areas. It is cultivated for its flowers and its fruit, which is popularly used to make jam, fruit tarts and cakes and huckleberry syrup.

Juniper Gardens   Juniper is a shrub or small tree growing to about 20 feet. Of the pine family, it has spine-tipped greyish 'needles' in whorls of three, and yellow flowers in May and June. Its berry-like fruit is green before turning blue-black when ripe and is used in the making of gin. Juniper grows in coniferous woods, moors, heaths, downs, mountains and cliffs.

Khasiaberry   The Khasia is a variety of palm tree which originated in the Himalayan regions of Nepal, India and Burma. It grows up to about 40 feet and has a tall, slim trunk and large upright, fan-shaped leaves of glossy green. It has white flowers and egg-shaped berries.

Lavender Grove   Lavender can grow up to three feet on woody stems. Its flowers range from purple through to blue, pink and white growing in spike formation. Its powerful, evocative scent is used in perfumery and sprigs of the dried flowers have long been used to scent clothes drawers and linen chests. In olden days it was put behind the ears to ease headaches. Today, lavender is commercially grown, particularly in Norfolk.

Lichfield Down   At a small village called Wall on the outskirts of Lichfield in Staffordshire, the two Roman roads, Watling Street and Ryknild Street, cross each other. By the 18th century they were important highways for both commercial and private travel. Lichfield was a busy stop-over city with many coaching inns; Lichfield Turnpike Trust was in charge of improving and maintaining the roads and collecting the tolls.

Meadowsweet   Meadowsweet is of the rose family. It is a tall perennial plant with leafy stems and flowers growing in dense clusters of creamy, fragrant petals from June to September. Meadowsweet grows in marshes, fens and swamps, wet meadows and woods.

Nutmeg Close   The nutmeg is an east Indian evergreen tree, cultivated in the tropics for its hard, aromatic seed, which is used as a spice. The aril, or seed covering, of the nutmeg is dried and used as mace. There is also the flowering nutmeg, which is a shrub growing to about six feet, with purplish flowers,

Paprika Court   Paprika is a mild powdered seasoning, or spice, made from the dried berries of a sweet variety of red pepper.

Parsley Court   Parsley is a herb, of which there are 13 varieties. The South European Parsley is best known and cultivated for its aromatic, curled leaves, used in cookery for flavouring white sauces and soups. The common, wild cow parsley is easily recognised growing in fields and road verges by its clusters of white flowers on tall stems. Horses and cattle are particularly partial to it.

Penny Royal   Penny Royal is a herb of the mint family. A few inches high, it has oval leaves, lilac flowers and is strongly aromatic. It flourishes from July to October in damp places.

Pettingrew Close   No information found.

Pimpernel Grove   This bright red little flower is common everywhere, in gardens, fields and waste places, but hard to find. Country folk gave it a reputation as a weather forecaster, as its petals close when rain is approaching although its habit is to close its petals anyway after about 2 p.m., whatever the weather. The pimpernel is an annual which lies along the ground, sending up many small stems with a little scarlet flower on the end of each, from May to November. There is also a blue variety.

Pinfold   The Walnut Tree area was in the parish of Walton, which once had two manors. Towards the end of the 17th century, one of the manors was bought by Sir Thomas Pinfold. He was Chancellor of the Diocese of Peterborough and Commissary of St Paul's. He died in 1701 and his monument is in Walton church. The manor then passed to his son, Dr Charles Pinfold, Provost of Eton and, after his death in 1754, to his son, Charles, who was Governor of Barbados 1755-6. He was succeeded in 1788 by his nephew, Captain Charles Pinfold. The word 'pinfold' means a pound or enclosure for cattle.

Plantain Court   Plantain, or Lamb's Tongue, is abundant in Britain, growing in dry pastures or waste places, mainly on limestone soil. There are several varieties of the plantain family. Growing among grasses, they have veined leaves with 'flower' heads on top of tall stalks.

Pomander Crescent   A pomander is a mixture of aromatic substances in a sachet, or contained in an orange skin. It was once carried as a scent, or as a protection against disease.

Quince Close   The quince is a shrub growing to about ten feet, or a tree growing to twenty. It has pointed, oval leaves, pink blossom and yellow fruit. The branches can grow in an odd, crooked fashion if not trained against a wall. The fruit is either pear- or apple-shaped with a sweet scent when ripe and is often cooked with apples to vary the taste. In olden times quince was used to make wine and today is used mostly to make jam or marmalade.

Ramsthorn Grove   This is another name for the common buckthorn. Of the family *Rhamnaceae*, it is a bushy shrub found in woods and near streams. It has small greenish-yellow flowers, followed by pea-sized black berries, which in Anglo-Saxon times were boiled with honey to make a laxative syrup. The berries were similarly used until the late 19th century.

Rockspray Grove   The rockspray cotoneaster is a horizontal-growing deciduous shrub with a low-growing, fishbone-branching style. It has small, shiny green leaves and pink flowers in spring. In late autumn, the leaves turn red and the shrub has bright red berries which remain through December. It is popularly grown in the United States of America.

Rosebay Close   The name rosebay pertains to any of several rhododendrons, or to the rosebay willowherb, which is a perennial plant that has spikes of deep pink flowers and is widespread in the northern hemisphere. Rosebay is also another name for the oleander.

Rosemary Court   Rosemary is a European ornamental evergreen shrub which grows up to five feet. It has spiky green leaves and pale blue flowers in early summer. In olden days, the dried leaves were scattered over floors in homes and churches as an air freshener and sometimes substituted for incense. Today rosemary is widely cultivated for its leaves, which are used in cookery and in the manufacture of perfume. It is the traditional flower of remembrance.

Samphire Court   The golden samphire is of the daisy family. It is a shortish perennial with narrow leaves growing upwards along the stem and small, yellow tufted flowers from July to October. It grows on coastal cliffs, shingle and salt marshes. The rock samphire, of the carrot family, is a greyish perennial with narrow, fleshy leaves and yellow flower bracts. It also grows on cliffs, rocks and sands by the sea from July to October.

Sandbriar Close   This is another name for the Jerusalem Cherry, or bittersweet (*Solanum dulcamara*). Of the nightshade family, it has bright red berries and the whole plant is highly poisonous.

Shamrock Close   The shamrock is the national emblem of Ireland. A three-leaved plant, there are different beliefs about its true identity. In popular tradition the shamrock is the lesser yellow trefoil; according to some English poets, it is the wood sorrel; while some say it is the white clover, others say it is the hop trefoil, black medick, or any three-leaved plant.

Silverweed Court   Silverweed is a creeping plant with long runners which put down more roots. It has silvery leaves and yellow flowers from May to August and grows in damp, grassy places. Another variety of silverweed does not creep and has smaller flowers growing in clusters in dry grassy places.

Spearmint Close   The spearmint is of the mint family. It is a sharply aromatic herb which can have either green and shiny or greyish coloured leaves. It has lilac flowers in a pointed spike and flourishes from July to October. It grows wild in damp, waste places but is commonly cultivated as garden mint. In the Middle Ages, spearmint was used to relieve digestive problems.

Studley Knapp   Studley in Warwickshire is just south of Redditch, on the A435 which links Redditch to Alcester. A turnpike trust was set up in 1754 to maintain the road and a toll-house was built in 1839 on the north side of Alcester at the junction of the roads to Studley (A435) and Droitwich (B4090). The toll-house was demolished in the mid-1940s. Knap means a protuberance, such as a hillock or hill-crest.

Tamarisk Court   Tamarisk is an evergreen shrub which grows to about ten feet and has twiggy, reddish-coloured stems, small, wispy foliage and pink flowers growing in stalked spikes. It flourishes from July to September by salt or fresh water and is often cultivated in gardens.

Tamworth Stub   Tamworth in Staffordshire is on the A5 Watling Street. Several roads radiating from Tamworth were turnpiked around 1760. On the Tamworth-Ashby turnpike stood the *Red Lion Inn*, where the 'Dart' stagecoach picked up and dropped its passengers. Stub probably indicates an area of land which was covered with stumpy bushes.

Tarragon Close   Tarragon is a south-west Asian plant, a tall, aromatic, all-green perennial with globular flowers in spikes of yellow-green from July to September. It grows wild or in gardens.

Tatling Grove   Tatling End is an area of Gerrards Cross, Buckinghamshire, which was a coaching stop on the main London to Oxford road (now the A40). When the road was turnpiked, the toll-gate was probably at Tatling.

Twin-Flower   The twin-flower is of the honeysuckle family. It is a delicate, prostrate evergreen undershrub, with small, oval leaves and bell-shaped, drooping flowers growing in pairs from June to August. It is very fragrant and grows in coniferous woods.

Twyford Lane   Twyford, near Reading, Berkshire, was on the old London to Bath road. The section between Twyford and Reading was turnpiked in

1736, but not without objections by the people of Reading who feared that their cattle market would suffer due to the tolls which the farmers would have to pay on each animal. The toll-gate at Twyford took £1,215 a year, and by 1806 17 coaches a day were passing through the turnpike.

Walton Road   This is part of the original country lane which ran between the villages of Wavendon and Walton, passing the gates of Walnut Tree Farm.

WALTON

Although one of the smallest of the 13 original villages incorporated in Milton Keynes, Walton was, perhaps, the most enchanting. St Michael's church, built around 1350, stood alone in a field beside a stream, guarded by handsome trees. Sharing the peace at a discreet distance was the 19th-century Walton Hall and, in the fields to the south, 16th-century Walton Manor, stable block and barns. A handful of cottages and the old rectory completed the picture. Now the village does not exist. The 760 acres which constituted the parish have been divided into three separate domains – Walton Hall, Walton and Walton Park. Despite its ancient history, Walton is not mentioned in Domesday Book but was recorded in 1189 as 'walled, or fenced about'. Therefore, its name possibly derives from the Anglo-Saxon w(e)ald or w(e)all and tun, meaning a farmstead in a forest, or with a wall.

THEME **Walton Parish History**

Walton

The locality now known as Walton covers the lands of **Walton Manor.** A listed 16th-century manor house with a 16th-century barn and 19th-century stable block, the Manor was for many years a stud farm until acquired by Milton Keynes Development Corporation and is now occupied by the veterinary medicines company, Intervet. Its historical owners include the Brays, the Greys and the Williams family before it was jointly owned with Walton Hall by the Gilpins, said to have been related to John Gilpin the highwayman. This is very unlikely as John Gilpin was the fictitious character in Cowper's ballad and was based on a London linen-draper named Beyer.

Walton Hall Open University Campus

One of the two Walton manors, the present part-18th-, part-19th-century Walton Hall is the centrepiece of the sprawling Open University campus. A much earlier, medieval, building on the site was owned in the 1200s by the

Walton Hall, pre-Open University.

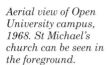

Aerial view of Open University campus, 1968. St Michael's church can be seen in the foreground.

Aerial view of Open University campus, Walton, 2004.

Rixbaud family before passing into the hands of the Hunts and then, by marriage, to the Longuevilles who, by the 16th century, had sold it to the Beales. By the end of the 17th century it had been bought by Sir Thomas Pinfold who pulled down most of the old building and replaced it with an early Georgian mansion which, in 1830, Captain Charles Pinfold partly replaced with the present neo-classical Walton Hall. Before being purchased by the Open University in 1970, the Hall and its grounds had been owned by the Earle family since 1932.

Church Lane This follows the line of the old lane leading from Milton Road to the church of St Michael.

Harley Hall The old village community centre, Harley Hall is named after Dr Vaughan Harley who purchased Walton Hall in 1907. He was an eminent heart specialist and descendant of Edward Harley, 2nd Earl of Oxford, who owned the land on which London's Harley Street was built and after whom it is named.

Milton Road This is a section of the original lane which led from Walton to the village of Milton Keynes.

Rectory Lane The Old Rectory, a listed 16th-century building with 18th- and 19th-century alterations, is now home to Ravenstone House Preparatory School.

St Michaels Drive A campus road passing St Michael's church, which has held its ground on this spot since 1350 although its outlook has drastically changed.

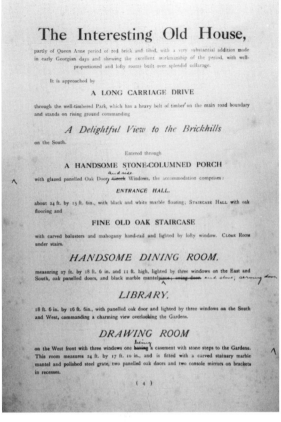

Page three of 'Particulars of Auction Sale of Walton Hall Estate' by Dr Vaughan Harley in 1911.

St Michael's church, Walton from a painting by local artist P. Yourell, September 1979.

After restoration by the Milton Keynes Development Corporation, the church was reopened in 1978 and is used by the university for concerts, exhibitions and occasional services. An archaeological dig found remnants of the church which stood here in 1189 with a 12th-century font, as well as medieval stained glass, floor tiles dated about 1500 and made at the local Brickhill kiln, and traders' tokens from the 1650s, when some restoration work was done by the Beales.

Walton Drive   This is the main driveway leading up to the Hall since it became the Open University.

WALTON PARK

Bartholomew Close   There is a monument to Bartholomew Beale, lord of the manor, in Walton church. It was erected in 1672 by his sons, Henry and Charles.

Beales Lane   Bartholomew Beale (1583-1660) bought the Walton Hall Manor from the Longuevilles in the 16th century. His younger son, Charles, a cloth manufacturer, married Mary Cradock who, as Mary Beale, became a renowned portrait painter. She had a studio in Covent Garden and among her sitters were Archbishop Tillotson, John Milton and Charles II. Theodore Beale was rector of St Michael's church, Walton from 1643 to 1652.

Chase Avenue   The Chase, an unenclosed parkland where game was kept for hunting, was granted in 1242 to John Fitzgeoffrey and passed to the Giffard family. It anciently covered 22,000 acres of land which included Shenley, Whaddon and Great Horwood.

Cook Close   In the late 19th century, David Cook, a farmer, shared ownership of the Walton lands with Fanny Maria Pinfold, granddaughter of Captain Charles Pinfold of Walton Hall. By 1915, David Cook had acquired most of the land, which he then shared with the Harley family.

Katherine Close   Katherine was the wife of Bartholomew Beale, lord of the manor of Walton Hall in the early 17th century. There is a monument to Katherine and her husband in Walton church.

Lightfoot Court   At Walton in the early 1800s, the *Angel Inn* was kept for many years by the Lightfoot family. By the end of the 19th century, William Lightfoot, a grazier, or cattle farmer, resided at the *Pine Tree* public house. Whether there were two inns at Walton is unclear. Possibly the name of the *Angel* was changed at some time.

Limbaud Close   Corrupted from the name of Godfrey de Limhoud who, in 1225, presented Roger de Bray to a moiety (part) of the parsonage. Limhoud is believed to have been a relative of the Brays.

Luttle Marsh   This is a modernisation of 'Lutlemers', which was the name of an area of marshy ground in Walton parish in the 13th century. The name possibly derives from the Old English *lytel* and *mersc,* meaning little marsh. With other lands, Lutlemers was granted by Robert de Boclande of Walton to Richard, son of Radulph Ane of Walton, on his marriage to Boclande's daughter, Armicia, in the 13th century. By the early 18th century, there were three meadows, Little March, North March and South March, which were probably part of the same area.

Pearse Grove   William Pearse was rector of the parish church of St Thomas the Apostle at the neighbouring village of Simpson in 1667-8.

Pyxe Court   On the north chancel wall of Walton church there is a commemorative brass epitaph to Elizabeth Pyxe, who died aged 11 years in 1617. She was the daughter of William Pyxe, rector of St Michael's, Walton between 1598 and 1642.

Redcote Manor   Redcote Manor was a third titular manor in the 13th century owned by the Redcote family. It passed through several hands before the Gilpins made it part of the whole estate.

Rixband Close. In about 1200, when Walton was first divided into two manors, the Rixbaud family held Walton Hall, while the Brays held Walton Manor. The Rixbauds remained in possession of the Hall for about a century.

Seagrave Court   The Seagrave family became members of the Pinfold family in the mid-19th century when a son of Captain Charles Pinfold married Anna Maria, daughter of the Rev. John Seagrave. A Miss Mary Seagrave seems to have been installed at Walton Hall as caretaker after the Pinfolds left in 1902. Miss Seagrave lived there until 1907 when the estate was sold to the Harleys.

Simpson Road   This is a section of the old road which, until the late 1970s, ran from Simpson to join what is now Brickhill Street, just south of Walton Manor.

Sturges Close   Arthur Sturges was a tenant farmer residing at Walton Manor at the end of the 19th century.

Wadesmill Lane. This lane connects Walton Park with Caldecotte and runs into Walnut Tree, thus taking up the turnpike theme. Wadesmill, near Ware in Hertfordshire, was the first turnpike with a toll-gate to be erected in the later 1600s. A small village beside the river Rib, its name suggests there was once a watermill here.

Williams Circle   The Williams family were granted the Redcote manor of Walton by the Crown in 1627, but soon afterwards it was acquired by the Beales.

Wingate Circle   George Wingate Pearse was rector of St Michael's church, Walton for nearly 50 years from 1851. He died on Boxing Day 1899.

WAVENDON GATE

Wavendon Gate adjoins the old village of Wavendon, which is not within the new city boundary. Known as Wafandun in 969 and recorded in Domesday Book as Wavendone, the name means 'hill of a man called Wafa'.

THEMES **(1) The Parish History of Wavendon and Walton (2) Lace-making, which was a thriving cottage industry in the Wavendon area**

Burano Grove   Burano is a type of lace which originated in the Venetian islet of Burano. At the beginning of the 15th century, Duchess Morosina Morosini gave her patronage to the Burano needlewomen enabling them to establish a workshop for 130 lace-makers. By the time the workshop closed, when the Duchess died, the fame of Burano lace had spread throughout Europe and its production continued well into the 20th century.

Coggeshall Grove   Coggeshall is a small, medieval Essex town renowned for wool and lace-making. Coggeshall lace is English Tambour hook lace, which is made on a circular frame.

Cluny Court   Cluny is a type of lace, taking its name from the town of Cluny in eastern France which is famous for its Benedictine abbey, founded in 910 and the centre of the Cluniac order of monks.

Denison Court   Mrs Denison had manorial rights in the third manor of Wavendon. In the 18th century, during the land enclosures, there were several claimants to this manor, but 'Mrs Denison's was the only estate entitled to an allotment on account of manorial rights' (*Magna Britannia 1806*). Mr Denison owned the principal manor and was Principal of Magdalen Hall, Oxford. Mrs Denison was a descendant of the Isaacson family.

Dixie Lane   At the beginning of the 19th century, the Dixie family were in possession of one of the three manors which existed in the Wavendon area.

Duchess Grove   Duchesse lace is a type of Flemish pillow lace with designs in cord outline. Developed in the mid-1800s from Brussels bobbin lace, in a larger format for speedier production, it is one of the most popular laces made today.

Flaxbourne Court   This may relate to the fact that flax was once widely grown in the fields around Wavendon and was used in lace-making. Bourne comes from the Old English *burna,* meaning a stream. There is a Flaxbourne Farm lying between nearby Salford and Aspley Guise.

Fortuna Court   A portrayal of Fortuna was found on the seal bearing the image of Mithras discovered at Wavendon Gate during excavations.

Fortuna, the Roman goddess of fortune and good luck, is usually depicted standing on a wheel distributing her favours from the cornucopia she holds in her hand.

Gable Thorne   Listed in the Walton Tithe Apportionment schedule of October 1839, Gable Thorn was pastureland of just over 25 acres. Also recorded in 1599 and 1625, Gablethorne furlong was then arable land in Walton parish. The *Victoria County History* for Buckinghamshire records it as 'Gabriel Thorn'.

Gaddesden Crescent   John de Gatesden, or Gaddesden, was lord of the manor of Little Brickhill in the early 13th century. He was the King's Physician and the first of several royal physicians to buy an estate in north Buckinghamshire.

Godwin Close   Earl Godwin of Wessex was father of King Harold and of Queen Edith, wife of Edward the Confessor. Edith owned the manors of Simpson and Milton Keynes during the 11th century, but in 1066 she betrayed both her brother and her local tenants by supporting William the Conqueror. After the Battle of Hastings, William's army, unable to enter London from the south, crossed the Thames at Wallingford and marched across north Buckinghamshire, destroying any resistance in its path. Simpson, Bow Brickhill, Milton Keynes, Woolstone and Wavendon were all devastated and the value of their lands was cut by half.

Gregories Drive   The Gregory family purchased The Grange manor house from the Thompson family sometime in the late 16th or early 17th century. Dipis Gregory is shown as a freeholder at Wavendon on the Buckingham Poll of 1784.

Honiton Court   The town of Honiton in east Devon is world-famous for the fine bobbin lace which was made there from the 16th century. Although no lace is made there on a commercial scale today, Honiton still maintains its tradition by catering for the many hundreds of people who practise lace-making as a hobby. Lace-making classes are held weekly and the Honiton Lace Shop is a mine of information and materials.

Isaacson Drive   The Isaacson family held the principal manor of Wavendon during the 18th century, after Robert Isaacson obtained it in 1735.

Lamb Lane   This probably refers to the Lamb family, local builders merchants who, in 1919, joined Messrs Read and Andrews to form the Bletchley Brick Company. Brickmaking had been a local industry for decades, with kilns in many areas now covered by Milton Keynes, including at Woburn Sands, Bow Brickhill and Wavendon, where there was also a limekiln.

Lester Court   Possibly named after John de Leycestre who held land at Walton 'abutting on stream at Alfladebro(u)ge' in 1296.

March Meadow   This was five acres of pastureland recorded in the Walton

Tithe Apportionment schedule of October 1839. In about 1710, North March and South March were listed as meadows in Walton parish.

Minerva Gardens   The Roman goddess Minerva is Patron of the Arts and Handicrafts and Goddess of Wisdom. In mythology, she sprang fully armed and with a tremendous battle cry from Jupiter's brain.

Mithras Gardens   A seal bearing the image of Mithras was found during excavations at Wavendon Gate. Mithra was the Persian God of Light who slayed a bull, the blood of which, it was believed, was the mainspring of all animal life. Known as Mithras by the Romans, the cult of Mithraism flourished during the second century AD, especially among the Roman legions who revered Mithras as the enemy of evil.

Norton Leys   William Norton was rector of St Mary's church, Wavendon 1608-48. In the Walton Tithe Apportionment schedule of 1839, Norton Leys is listed as 36 acres of pasture.

Ortensia Drive   This drive leads to Wavendon Tower. Ortensia was an Italian countess married to Henry Burney, the first owner of Wavendon Tower, which became the headquarters of the Milton Keynes Development Corporation.

Passalewe Lane   The principal manor of Wavendon was held by the Passalewes from 1180 to 1313. Nicholas Passalewe was also lord of the manor of Mursley and Lord of Drayton. In 1345 he drew up a formal agreement with two other local lords to change from the two-field system to the three-field system of agriculture. Very few landowners of the time agreed with these changes. Known as the Mursley-Dunton Agreement, the document was drawn up in French and is unique. Nicholas Passalewe and all his tenants died when the Black Death hit Mursley in 1348.

Saunders Close   In St Mary's church, Wavendon there are memorials to the Saunders family of Battlesden. Richard Saunders died in 1639 having fathered 27 children by four different wives. He also held the Redcote manor of Walton, which he acquired from Thomas Anglesey and later sold to Thomas Gilpin. There was also a lace-maker called Saunders in Wavendon during the 17th century.

Scotch Firs   In about 1778, Wavendon Heath, which is a large tract of Aspley Heath adjacent to Woburn Sands, was planted with 51,376 Scotch firs, by Francis Moore of Eggington, Bedfordshire. By 1794, after thinning out, 17,124 of the trees remained.

Shuttleworth Grove   Historically, the Wavendon manorial estate was divided into three portions, one of which was bought by a Mr Shuttleworth in the 18th century.

Sipthorp Close. A Mr W. Sipthorp is listed in the 1784 Buckinghamshire Poll as living at nearby Simpson in property belonging to Campbell Goodman. With a very similar name, John Sibthorpe was a councillor on the first

Fenny Stratford Urban District Council when local councils were first set up in the second half of the 19th century. The Sibthorpes were a long-established local family of tenant farmers renting lands at Shenley during the 1770s.

Stevens Field   Stevens Field was arable land of about 18 acres belonging to William Stevens, recorded in the Posse Comitatus as a Grazier of Walton in 1798. Ann Stevens, possibly his sister, is also recorded as owning five horses, three carts and one wagon. By 1839, the Tithe Apportionment schedule for Walton lists a five-acre field called Stevens Home Close and Stevens Homestead, in addition to Stevens Field.

Taranis Close   Taranis was a Celtic god, equivalent to the Romans' Jupiter. During excavations before the building of Wavendon Gate, a solar wheel, symbol of Taranis, was found at Wavendon.

Trumpton Lane   Upper Trumpton and Lower Trumpton were glebe land owned by Thomas Austin Plowman. They are listed in the 1839 Tithe Apportionment schedule for Walton, as are Trumptons Close and Lower Trump.

Venetian Court   Venetian needlepoint lace originated in the 16th century in and around Venice and the Venetia region of Italy.

Walton End   This is a short strip of the old lane which ran between Wavendon and Walton.

WILLEN

Willen is the name of an existing village and comes from the Anglo-Saxon meaning 'at the place of the willows'. Its main feature of interest is the church of St Mary Magdalene, built in the style of Wren by Robert Hooke at the instigation of Dr Richard Busby in 1680. Since Dr Busby played such a major part in the village's history, it is surprising that no road bears his name. Although Busby and Hooke would recognise their church today from the outside, they might be appalled by the destructive internal alterations which have taken place over the years. In 1814 the Cupola was removed. In 1862 a new apse was built and stained-glass windows installed, but Dr Busby's organ, which the church was built to house, was replaced by a Victorian organ, also replaced during a major renovation in the 1970s. The reredos attributed to Grinling Gibbons has gone, and plain glass has replaced the Victorian stained-glass windows which are now in store at Ely Cathedral. No attempt has ever been made at restoration and this once beautiful, historic church has been stripped of its air of sanctity. Dr Busby died a rich man, but he failed to leave anything for the maintenance of his church of St Mary Magdalene at Willen.

THEME The History of the Parish

Aldrich Drive   Dr Henry Aldrich (1647-1710), a Busby Trustee, was an English cleric. He attended Westminster School and Christ Church, Oxford, of which he became a canon in 1682 and Dean in 1689. He was also an architect and designed the college's Peckwater Quadrangle.

Amherst Court   Earl Amherst was a Busby Trustee in 1857, as was William Pitt, Earl Amherst, between 1869 and 1886.

Bates Close   Mr William Bates was one of the craftsmen employed in the building of Robert Hooke's church of St Mary Magdalene, Willen. Listed in Dr Busby's accounts as a carpenter, he built the font, the cover of which is by Grinling Gibbons. Bates was also employed by Sir Christopher Wren in the rebuilding of the church of St Anne and St Agnes, Gresham Street, London after it was badly damaged in the Great Fire of London.

Beaufort Drive   Henry, Lord Carleton, Duke of Beaufort was a Busby Trustee. The title Duke of Beaufort was first bestowed in 1682 on Henry Somerset, the son of the Marquess of Worcester. During Tudor and Stuart times they were courtiers, and the family seat was, and still is, Badminton House, Gloucestershire. Henry, the 7th Duke (1792-1853) and his son Henry, the 8th Duke (1824-99) were keen sportsmen, the latter helping to devise the game of badminton, named after the house, in about 1870.

Bentall Close   The Reverend John Benthall was vicar of Willen from 1852 until his death in 1887, aged 81. Born in 1806 in Totnes, Devon, he attended Westminster School, where he was a gifted scholar, and after studying at Trinity College, Cambridge, returned to his old school as a teacher. It seems that he was badly affected by the premature death of his wife, and was dismissed from Westminster for failing to maintain discipline. He is said to have been a devout, compassionate and learned man who lived quietly, writing religious books, although the mid-years of his life were interrupted by scandal and personal tragedy. Behind the altar of the church there are paintings by his daughter, Louisa Benthall, depicting the original reredos. In the entrance porch is a memorial plaque to several members of the Benthall family.

Carleton Gate   Henry, Lord Carleton, Duke of Beaufort was a Busby Trustee 1724-5.

Carteret Close   John, Lord Carteret, who became Earl Granville, was a Busby Trustee.

Chillery Leys   This was the name of a field, occupied by Thomas Chelerey, a Willen householder and probably a farmer, in 1522.

Christian Court   John Christian was vicar of the old church of St Mary Magdalene, Willen from 1501 to 1540. The old church, which had been built by the Normans, had fallen into a state of disrepair by the 17th century, when Dr Busby had it demolished in order to build his new church, designed by Robert Hooke, in its place.

Corbett Close   This most probably refers to Corbett Scriven (see Scriven Court). Another possibility is William Corbett, rector of nearby Holy Trinity church, Little Woolstone from 1794.

Dolben Court   Sir Gilbert Dolben (1658-1722) was a Busby Trustee. The eldest son of Dr Dolben, Archbishop of York, Sir Gilbert was a Judge, and MP for Ripon in 1685. He was made Justice of the Common Pleas in Ireland in 1701 and created a Baronet in 1704.

Drummond Hay   Robert Auriol Drummond-Hay, Earl of Kinnoul, Viscount Dupplin of Dupplin, Baron Hay of Kinfauns in Scotland and also Baron Hay of Pedwardin in Hereford, was a Busby Trustee. He was born in March 1751, married first in 1791 a Nottinghamshire girl who died within two years, then Sarah, daughter of the 3rd Earl of Oxford, who bore him two children.

Dr Richard Busby, 17th-century lord of the manor of Willen. He commissioned Robert Hooke to build the church of St Mary Magdalene in 1678.

Granville Square   A Busby Trustee, John Carteret, 1st Earl Granville (1690-1783), was a statesman, orator and diplomat. Son of Baron Carteret, he studied at Westminster School and Christ Church, Oxford and became a Lord of the Bedchamber to George I. After a long and colourful political career, which included the Lord Lieutenancy of Ireland, he was appointed Earl Granville after accompanying George II at the Battle of Dettingen in 1743. Also a Busby Trustee, from 1770 to 1804, was Granville, Earl Gower, who became Marquess of Stafford.

Grimbald Court   Hugh Grimbald in 1208-9 held half a virgate (about 15 acres) of land in Willen by enfeoffment (in return for military service). In 1210, he is recorded as holding land belonging to Rose Verdon.

Hooper Gate   Dr George Hooper was a Trustee of Dr Busby's charity. He was Dean of Canterbury and, later, Bishop of Bath and Wells.

Ketton Close   The stone used in the building of the church of St Mary Magdalene came from the quarries at Ketton, near Rutland. In Dr Busby's hand-written accounts for the church, Ketton stone was obtained from someone called Manning.

Landsborough Gate   Lord Viscount Landsborough was a Trustee of the charitable organisation known as the Busby Trust. This was set up by Dr Richard Busby, who was lord of the manor of Willen 1673-95 and a headmaster of Westminster School. It was he who commissioned Robert Hooke to design Willen church and paid for the building of it. The Trust inaugurated by his Will ensured that the church would continue to maintain its links with Westminster School by stipulating that Trustees must be old boys and they should select as vicars men who had been educated at Westminster and attended Christ Church, Oxford.

Linford Lane   In the old village of Willen, this is a section of the road which once led to Linford but now trails onto a redway (cycle track).

Millington Gate   Sir Thomas Millington was a Busby Trustee. He was President of the Royal College of Physicians in 1696. Appropriately, this road is on the site of a field known as Old Miller's Ground.

Milton Road   This is a section of the lane which once linked Willen with Milton Keynes village.

Newport Road   This is a section of the old road which linked Simpson to Newport Pagnell, passing through several of the villages now incorporated in Milton Keynes. Its course can still be traced, as much of it has been retained in lengths of either road or footpath.

Oaktree Court   This is the name of a sheltered housing development, which was trumpeted in 1988 as 'the first of its kind in the City, offering high-class homes for the elderly' (*Milton Keynes Citizen*), and presumably so called because of the presence of an oak tree.

Portland Drive   The Duke of Portland was a Busby Trustee in 1765. This was William Cavendish, 3rd Duke (1738-1809), a statesman who succeeded Lord Rockingham as leader of the Whig party, and went on to serve twice as Prime Minister, in 1783 and from 1807-9.

Roslyn Court   It has been suggested that 'lyn' was added to the name of William Lennox Lascelles Fitzgerald, 23rd Baron de Ros, who was a Busby Trustee in the 19th century.

Scriven Court   Corbett Whitton Adkins Scriven was born at Willen House in 1840. There is a marble memorial plaque to him and his wife, Susan, above the choir of the church. There was also a local farmer called George Scriven.

Smabridge Walk   Believed to be a misprint of the possibly intended Smalridge. Dr George Smalridge, Bishop of Bristol, was nominated a Busby Trustee in 1701.

The Hooke   Leading to the church of St Mary Magdalene, this lane is named after Robert Hooke, architect of the church. Hooke was a pupil at Westminster School where Dr Busby was his housemaster. He went on to Christ Church, Oxford and later became Professor of Geometry at Gresham College, London. A brilliant physicist and instrument maker, he invented the quadrant, a marine barometer, a microscope, and a pocket watch. His surveying and architectural skills came to prominence after the Great Fire of London in 1666, when he was appointed Surveyor for the City of London, and worked with Sir Christopher Wren on the designs for many London buildings. Dr Busby's commission for the rebuilding of Willen church brought Robert Hooke to Willen several times between 1678 and 1680 for discussions with Dr Busby and the craftsmen involved in the project, which usually took place over dinner with wine. Memorial tablets to Hooke and Busby lie close to each other at the foot of the sacrarium in Westminster Abbey.

Thursby Close   William Thursby was a Busby Trustee. He was a distinguished lawyer who purchased and lived in part of the Hanslope estate, which he acquired from Dr Francis Turner, Bishop of Ely.

Tuffnell Close   John Tuffnell was a stonemason who worked on the building of St Mary Magdalene church.

The Church of St Mary Magdalene, Willen.

Wellfield Court   Wellfield is mentioned in terriers of 1639. Well Hill was the name of a large field recorded in a survey of lands in the Lordship of Dr Richard Busby in 1690 as lying in the west of Willen parish and farmed by Humphrey Sampson.

WILLEN LAKE

Willen Lake is disected by the H5 Portway grid-road into two halves, north lake and south lake, connected only by a very narrow neck on the east side. The largest area of water in Milton Keynes, the lakes were created in the early 1970s to collect rainwater off the city's streets and thereby prevent flooding. The north lake, a peaceful area, is overlooked by Willen Hospice, Willen Priory, the Japanese Peace Pagoda and the Buddhist Temple of Nipponzan Myohoji. The Pagoda was built by the monks and nuns of the temple and contains sacred relics of the Lord Buddha. There is also a a bird hide from which to watch an abundance of waterfowl including redshank, wigeon, terns and a variety of geese.

The south lake, known as Lakeside Park, is given over to watersports, fishing, horse riding, walking and family enjoyment. There are picnic areas, a lakeside hotel and restaurant, a miniature railway, boat hire facilities and a watersports centre.

WILLEN PARK

Abraham Close   In the church of St Mary Magdalene, there is a memorial above the pulpit to E.G. Abraham, who died during the Second World War while serving as an RAF Volunteer Reserve with the Bedfordshire and Hertfordshire regiment.

Bells Meadow   This is the name of a field, shown on a map of Willen in 1822.

Hammond Crescent   Colonel Robert Hammond bought Willen Manor in about 1653 from the Nichols family. A Parliamentarian during the Civil Wars, he was described by Oliver Cromwell as 'a valiant spirit'. He was appointed to Colonel Massie's Garrison Regiment of Horse at Gloucester and led the Parliamentary troops which captured Tewkesbury. On retiring from the army in about 1646 he was made Governor of the Isle of Wight, and when the King sought refuge there in 1647 Hammond was ordered to hold him prisoner in Carisbrooke Castle. Hammond died in 1654, thus escaping the fate of the Regicides after the Restoration. His wife, Mary, sixth daughter of the famous John Hampden, was allowed to keep Willen Manor under the Act of Oblivion. Their daughters, Mary and Letitia, sold it in 1673 to Dr Busby.

Hobart Crescent   After the death in 1654 of Colonel Robert Hammond, his widow Mary married Sir John Hobart, 3rd Baronet. In 1672, Hobart and Mary conveyed Willen Manor to Herbert Thornedicke and Barnabas Clay, clerks, in preparation for its sale by Elizabeth Hammond, Sir Edward and Mary Massie and Phineas and Letitia Preston, the three daughters of Colonel Hammond.

The Japanese Peace Pagoda at Willen.

Japonica Lane   Japonica is a Japanese shrub, also known as Japanese quince. In what may be termed the Japanese corner of Milton Keynes, this lane leads to the building which was, until it was recently demolished, the Gyosei Japanese boarding school. Also here in Willen Park is the Japanese Peace Pagoda, built by Buddhist monks and nuns of the Nipponzan Myohoji sect in the late

The city in the country – feeding the ducks at Willen Lake by the Wayfarer Hotel. Willen is one of a network of balancing lakes and is also a centre for leisure and recreation.

1970s. Within it are kept the sacred relics of the Lord Buddha. In a corner of the park are a Japanese garden and a Buddhist temple, also built by the monks and nuns.

Massie Close   Sir Edward Massie married Col. Hammond's other daughter, Mary. With their sister, Elizabeth, the three daughters sold Willen to Dr Busby in 1673. Lieutenant Colonel Edward Massie (1619-74) was a soldier in the King's army prior to the outbreak of the first Civil War, when he switched to the Parliamentarian side. He commanded the Gloucester garrison in 1643 against the King's army, but seems to have been something of a 'double-agent'. Apparently changing sides and imprisoned several times during the wars, Massie was MP for Gloucester in 1660 and rewarded by Charles II with the Governorship of Jamaica.

Peterborough Gate   The Mordaunt family, Earls of Peterborough, were lords of the manor of Willen from 1490-1640. In 1637, John Mordaunt, Earl of Peterborough, conveyed the manor to his three sisters, Elizabeth, Margaret and Anne, but in 1641 he relinquished his claim to the Nicholls family.

Phillimore Close   George Phillimore was vicar of the church of St Mary Magdalene, Willen in 1832. Other Phillimores were Busby Trustees: Joseph Phillimore Esq. DCL between 1840 and 1885, the Rt Hon. Sir Robert Joseph Phillimore in 1886 and Sir Walter George F. Phillimore Bart in 1885.

Preston Court   Phineas Preston was the husband of Letitia, daughter of Col Robert Hammond.

Shipman Court   Malcolm Parker Shipman was vicar of St Mary Magdalene 1928-35.

Skipton Close   Daniel Skipton AM (sometimes recorded as Shipton), of Christ Church, Oxford, was vicar of Willen church for 40 years from 1766 until his death in 1805. He was also rector of Wavendon and Master of the North Bucks Hounds.

Verdon Drive   The Verdon (or de Verduns) family were lords of the manor of Willen from about 1205, when it was held by Rose de Verdon, until the 1390s. In about 1285, Robert Verdon married Alice Maunsell of Shenley, without her guardian's consent. Alice's sister, Mabel, was married to Richard de la Vache, whose family had succeeded the Maunsells as lords of the Shenley estates. Disputes between the Vaches and the Verdons over the ownership of Shenley lands led to a law suit, which was eventually settled by the two sisters and their husbands agreeing to divide Shenley between them.

Whitsun Pasture   'Little Whitson Pasture' was the name of a field divided in two, one half being shared by John Kilpin and Thomas Chad and the other farmed by Humphrey Sampson. 'Great Whitson Pasture' was a large field in the east of the parish, farmed by George Chapman. All are identified on a 1690 Survey of the Manor of Willen, being the Lordship of Dr Richard Busby.

Willen Park Avenue   Connects this area with Willen village.

SELECT BIBLIOGRAPHY

AA Book of British Villages, Drive Publications Ltd, 1980

AA Illustrated Guide to Britain, Drive Publications Ltd, 1971

Bunney, Sarah (ed.), *The Illustrated Book of Herbs*, Octopus Books Ltd, 1984

Chambers Biographical Dictionary, W & R Chambers Ltd, 1986

Coincraft's 1997 Standard Catalogue of English and UK Coins, 1066-date

Hindley, Geoffrey (ed.), *Larousse Encyclopaedia of Music*, Hamlyn Publishing Group, 1978

Hudson's Historic Houses and Gardens, Norman Hudson & Company, 2002

Markham, Sir Frank, *History of Milton Keynes and District*, White Crescent Press, 1973

Osborne, Charles (ed.), *The Dictionary of Composers*, The Bodley Head, 1977

Peplow, Elizabeth and Reginald, *In a Monastery Garden*, David & Charles, 1988

Ward, John Owen (ed.), *The Oxford Companion to Music*, 10th edition, 1970

Useful Websites

Medieval Abbeys and Monasteries in England: www.britainexpress.com

Villages in Kent and East Sussex: www.villagenet.co.uk

Illustration acknowledgements:

Buckinghamshire Archives, pages 17, 53, 91; Dankworth Management, page 64; *Milton Keynes Gazette*, pages 49 (left), 82 (top); MK Local Studies Centre, page 77; National Portrait Gallery, London, page 50; Open University Archives, pages 82 (middle and bottom), 83 (top). Other photographs are by the author.